Best Pub Walks
around
CHESTER & THE DEE VALLEY

John Haywood

Published by Sigma Leisure – an imprint of
Sigma Press, 1 South Oak Lane, Wilmslow, Cheshire SK9 6AR, England.

British Library Cataloguing in Publication Data
A CIP record for this book is available from the British Library.

ISBN: 1-85058-471-0

Typesetting and Design by: Sigma Press, Wilmslow, Cheshire.

Cover photograph: The Swan Inn, Marbury *(photo: T. Heathcote).*

Maps and photographs: J. Haywood

Printed by: MFP Design & Print

Preface

The people of Chester and the Dee valley are lucky in having a marvellous variety of walking country within little more than half an hour's drive of their homes: I hope the selection of walks in this book fully reflects that variety. They include such diverse environments as the salt-marshes of the Dee estuary, the sandstone hills and reedy meres of Cheshire, the limestone cliffs of the Eglwyseg, the high heather moors of the Clwydian Hills and lush pastures beside the Dee. Besides beautiful scenery, the walks also take in many sites of great historical interest, including caves inhabited by Palaeolithic man, Iron Age hill forts, Dark Age ramparts, medieval castles, churches and bridges and mouldering reminders of the Industrial Revolution. To enhance your enjoyment, each walk is provided with background notes describing the points of historical, folklore, natural history and geological interest.

All the walks are circular and all but one start at, or within a few hundred yards of, a pub. The keen drinker will be pleased to find that many of the walks also take in one or two pubs along the way. All of the pubs included in the book serve food and all but one serves at least one cask-conditioned ale. Full details of opening hours, times that food is served, type of menu, beers served, availability of car parking and the landlord's attitude to children are given for each pub.

A sketch map is supplied for every walk. These are intended to amplify the directions given in the text, however, they are not drawn to scale and so should not be seen as substitutes for the Ordnance Survey 1:50,000 Landranger or 1:25,000 Pathfinder maps. Details are also given of how to get to the start of the walk from Chester and Wrexham by car and, where it is possible, public transport.

The twenty walks described in this book vary in length from 4 miles to 8 miles and though most are fairly undemanding about a quarter do involve some steep ascents and descents and are quite strenuous. Stout waterproof footwear is recommended for all of the walks but is especially important in the Clwyd hills. All of the routes follow public rights of way or paths for which access agreements have been negotiated. At the time of writing all of the routes were clear of obstructions. If you do find that any path has been blocked, report it to the appropriate County Council: it only takes a telephone call.

John Haywood

Contents

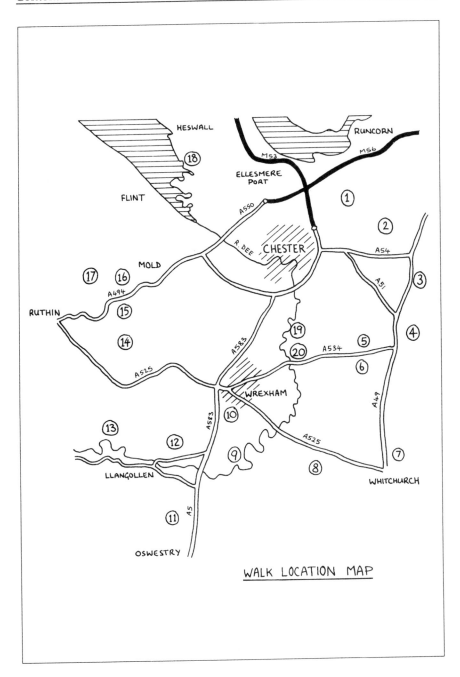

WALK LOCATION MAP

1. The sandstone edges above Helsby and Frodsham

Distance: Allow 4½ hours for this 7½ mile walk (3½ hours for the 5 mile version).

Maps: Landranger 1:50,000 – 117; Pathfinder 1:25,000 – 757 (SJ 47/57)

Map reference of start/finish: 497740

How to get there

From Chester: Leave Chester on the A56 heading for Helsby. Turn right at the traffic lights at the junction with the A5117, opposite the Helsby Arms pub. Turn right again almost immediately on the road signposted to Alvanley and Manley. Follow it uphill to a T-junction and turn right again (signposted to Alvanley and Manley). After about 300 yards you will come to another junction: head straight on and the White Lion is 200 yards further on the right. There is also limited roadside parking a bit further down the road, opposite Rose Cottage Gardens.

Public Transport: Arrowebrook service C76 has one bus a day (Mon-Fri) to Alvanley but this leaves only 3¾ hours to complete the walk and have a pub lunch before getting the return bus. Therefore it is probably better to start at Frodsham or Helsby which can easily be reached from Chester by the frequent services 20 and C31 (Mon-Sat).

From Wrexham: Take the A483 from Wrexham as far as the Chester by-pass and turn right. Keep on the by-pass as far as the junction with the A56 (signposted for Chester and Helsby). Turn right here in the direction of Helsby and follow the A56 for about 5 miles to the traffic lights at the junction with the A5117, opposite the Helsby Arms pub. Turn right here and right again almost immediately on the road signposted to Alvanley and Manley. Follow it uphill to a T-junction and turn right again (signposted to Alvanley and Manley). After about 300 yards you will come to another junction: head straight on and the White Lion is 200 yards further on the right. There is also limited roadside parking a bit further down the road, opposite Rose Cottage Gardens.

The White Lion

The White Lion, Alvanley

A whitewashed pub built around 1700 with a large car park where walkers may leave their cars if they are using the pub as well. Children are welcome in the lounge until 20.30 if eating and at all times in the beer garden which has a play area and a pets corner. Opening hours are 11.30-15.00 and 17.30-23.00 Monday-Saturday and 12.00-14.00 and 19.00-22.30 on Sundays. Beers include cask-conditioned Greenall's Original, Bitter and Mild and Young's Bitter and Theakston's Bitter as regular guests, plus a range of lagers including low alcohol brews on draught. The pub has an extensive menu which is changed regularly. Typical meals include steak and kidney pie, chicken curry, salmon steak in prawn sauce, rump steak and several vegetarian options. Food is served 12.00-14.00 and 18.00-21.30 Monday-Saturday and 12.00-14.30 and 19.00-21.30 on Sundays.

Helsby Hill

Background

The main interest of this walk lies in the splendid views to be had from the sandstone escarpments of Helsby Hill, Woodhouse Hill and Overton Hill which rise abruptly from the drained marshlands of the Mersey estuary. These are part of the low ridge of sandstone hills which stretches across Cheshire from Halton near Runcorn to Malpas over 20 miles to the south. Bedrock is never far below the surface on these hills and there are many interesting rock formations on this walk and on Helsby Hill there are cliffs of over 150 ft in height. Many of these rock faces, such as at Jacob's Ladder, have good examples of a geological feature known as current bedding. This has the appearance of oblique striations and are signs that these sandstones were laid down in shallow fast flowing water. When these rocks were laid down in the Triassic period, around 220 million years ago, Cheshire was a hot inland desert basin inhabited only by a few giant reptiles. Seasonal flood waters rushed down from the surrounding mountains spreading thick deposits of sand and pebbles over the plain. In some areas these inundations created short-lived lakes which evaporated to leave behind the salt deposits which have made such a contribution to Cheshire's prosperity.

These hills have long been valued as vantage points and were one of the first areas of Cheshire to have been inhabited by humans. Flint tools of prehistoric hunter-gatherers, dating to the Mesolithic period (c. 10,000-5,000 years ago) have been found on the hills above Frodsham. However, man's impact on the landscape was transient until the forts on Helsby Hill and Woodhouse Hill were built, probably by Celtic settlers around 2200 years ago. The fort on Helsby Hill has two earthwork ramparts and is, thanks to its cliff-top position, by far the most impressive of the two. It must have been even more impressive when first built for in those days the sea came almost to the base of the hill. The fort on Woodhouse Hill has a single rampart and was also protected on the south and west sides by low cliffs. The remains are supposed to be best preserved on the east side but the site is now so thickly wooded that little can be seen of them.

The walk starts at the village of Alvanley and touches the outskirts of two more, Helsby and Frodsham. All three are ancient settlements and feature in the Domesday Book. Alvanley is a small, quiet village situated on the crest of the sandstone ridge. Until the 18th century a fire dance, where the villagers leapt through the flames of a bonfire, was held in the village every spring and autumn. This was possibly a survival of the ancient Celtic festivals of Beltane and Samuin (which survives as Guy Fawkes' Night) which marked the end and the beginning of winter. More recently the custom of 'Roping' was practised. A rope was stretched across the church gate at weddings and the newly-weds had to pay for the locals to drink their health in the pub before being allowed to pass.

There is nothing notable about the large village of Helsby but its name which indicates a Danish connection. Place-names with the suffix 'by' – Old Danish for homestead – are common in the counties of eastern England which formed the Danelaw in the 10th century but they are uncommon in Cheshire. The name probably means 'homestead by the hill'.

Frodsham is a small town rather than a village and holds a weekly market which dates back to the 11th century. Frodsham's parish church was first founded in the Anglo-Saxon period but the oldest parts of the present church are Norman in style and date to c. 1170. The wide main street (wide to accommodate the market) has a number of 17th century buildings including the red sandstone stone Bear's Paw Inn built in 1632. Part of the pub's cellar was originally built as a boat-house so close did the Mersey come to the town in those days. Indeed, from the Middle Ages to the 18th century Frodsham was an important port for the export of Cheshire's two most famous products, salt and cheese. The Mersey has since receded, partly through silting up and partly through land drainage and reclamation of salt-marsh. Frodsham marshes are, though, still an important wintering ground for wildfowl.

The Walk

Start the walk at the public footpath which leaves the north side of the B5393 road alongside Rose Cottage Gardens about 50 yards SE of the White Lion. Follow the clearly marked field path through to Commonside Lane, turn right, then left when you reach the cross-roads (signposted to Frodsham) and about 100 yards after passing the caravan site take the wide path on the left-hand side of the road. The path soon narrows and twists and turns through bracken and then pastures before reaching a metalled lane. Turn left and follow the lane uphill all the way to the end, just past Harmers Lake Farm. Cross the stile to the right (signposted 'to summit'), through the low overgrown ramparts of the hill fort to the trig. point on the airy summit of Helsby Hill (462ft/141m). This is a splendid viewpoint: the peaks of Snowdonia and the Bowland Fells north of Preston can be seen in clear weather. However, it is the view of the Mersey estuary with its bustling activity and heavy industry that will hold the eye.

To pick up the descent route, walk from the trig point towards the green painted gate (but don't go through it) and the path will be seen bearing off to the left, through trees and giving good views of the sandstone cliffs on the hill's NW face. After about half a mile, the descending path meets a broad contour path. Turn right along this for a short distance to a stile on the edge of the woods. Take the grassy left-hand path downhill through gorse and past low cliffs to the road, then turn right and right again into Bates Lane. About 100 yards up the lane, take the narrow gated footpath round the back of the housing estate, across a field to an unmade road. The path now squeezes tightly between hedges to the right-hand side of 'Rose-mead', then across another field to reach a narrow lane at a miniature ford. Cross the ford – easily stepped across but a footbridge is provided – and walk up the lane to the Tarvin road. Turn left and almost immediately right up the drive to 'The Holt'.

At the top of the drive, go through the stile into the woods, recently bought by the Woodland Trust, a woodland conservation organisation. If you are doing the shorter version of the walk follow the sign for Woodhouse Hill steeply uphill to join the main route again at the SW corner of the hillfort. The main route heads for Frodsham and for the next mile the path runs through the edge of the woods keeping a fairly level course at the base of the hills until a stone staircase is reached. Climb it and at the top turn left onto a broad path. When the path turns into a road at 'Green Rigg' house, take the unmade road on the right, past a few houses and then uphill back into the woods. At the crest of the rise (by the black gate of Erindale Cottage) take the right-hand fork of the path, uphill at first but soon levelling out. This path eventually runs out into a residential street but just before it does take the steep uphill path on the right (almost doubling back on yourself).

The war memorial on Overton Hill soon appears above you and, as soon as the path levels off, make a bee-line for it by scrambling straight up the steep and rocky slope in front of you. There is a fine view from the memorial but the top, once graced by a helter-skelter, is now spoiled by the unlovely 'Mersey View Country Club' (how do these things get planning permission?). If you don't fancy scrambling up to the memorial, stay on the lower path which contours easily through woods to rejoin the main route near the top of Jacob's Ladder about 500 yards further on.

From the memorial a path runs between the boundary fence of the country club on one side and cliffs on the other. This path is

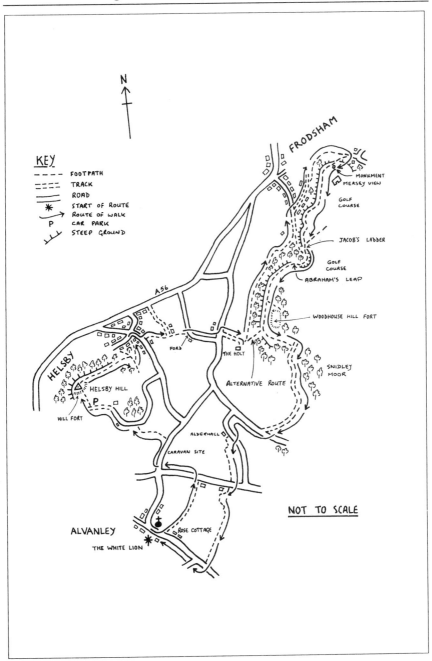

N

KEY

- - - - FOOTPATH
= = = = TRACK
——— ROAD
✳ START OF ROUTE
↷ ROUTE OF WALK
P CAR PARK
⊥⊥⊥ STEEP GROUND

FRODSHAM

MONUMENT
MERSEY VIEW

GOLF COURSE

JACOB'S LADDER

GOLF COURSE

ABRAHAM'S LEAP

WOODHOUSE HILL FORT

A56

FORD

THE HOLT

SNIDLEJ MOOR

ALTERNATIVE ROUTE

HELSBY

HELSBY HILL

P

HILL FORT

ALDERHALL

CARAVAN SITE

NOT TO SCALE

ALVANLEY

ROSE COTTAGE

THE WHITE LION

very narrow in some places and is probably not suitable for very young children. After about 500 yards the top of Jacob's Ladder is reached. This is a rough staircase cut in the face of a 50 ft cliff and its descent will not be enjoyed by those who lack a head for heights. Fortunately, the ladder has been by-passed by a new path which brings you down to its foot without any difficulty. This attractive cliff girt hollow is Dunsdale and the way out is along a wide ledge which crosses a low rock face known as Abraham's Leap.

The path continues along the wooded edge of the escarpment to a clearing where a good view over to Helsby Hill can be had from the top of low cliffs. At this point the Sandstone Trail branches off uphill to the right and goes around the east side of Woodhouse Hill fort. The fort site is thickly overgrown and its remains are not at all obvious (well, not to my eye at least!). Follow the Sandstone Trail if you like but a better idea of the natural strength of the site can be got by continuing straight on around the western and southern sides of the fort and turn right when the path rejoins the Sandstone Trail. Follow the Sandstone Trail, which becomes a deeply sunken lane, for half a mile down to a road.

Turn right here and walk down the road to Burrows Lane. Go down the lane and take the second footpath that you come to (just past 'Alderhall') across the fields to another lane. Just across the lane (slightly to your left) is another stile: cross it and follow the path along the edges of two small fields around the back of Bowlingalley Farm (nice duckpond). You cross another small field, over a stile and into a large field: aim for the solitary ash tree on the other side and on reaching the hedge turn left for a few yards to find a stile into an even larger field. Aim for the isolated oak trees in the middle of the field and continue in the same line to reach the B5393 about ¼ mile SE of the starting point.

2. Through Delamere Forest to the Black Lake

Distance: Allow 3 hours for this 5¾ mile walk

Maps: Landranger 1:50,000 – 117. Pathfinder 1:25,000 – 757 (SJ 47/57)

Map reference of start/finish: SJ 554722

How to get there

From Chester: Take the A51(T) to Tarvin, then the A54(T) and A556(T) in the direction of Northwich as far as the junction with the B5152 at the Vale Royal Abbey Arms. Turn left here and continue in the direction of Frodsham for just over two miles to Hatchmere village. About 200 yards past the shop/cafe at the crossroads is the Carriers Inn and, opposite, a large car park and picnic area with toilets.
Public transport: BR Chester to Delamere Station and join the route at the forest visitor centre 400 yards west. Services are about every 1-2 hours, depending on the time of day.

From Wrexham: Take the A483(T), then the A55(T), Chester by-pass, coming off on the A51(T), Northwich road. At Tarvin turn onto the A54(T) and A556(T) still in the direction of Northwich as far as the junction with the B5152 at the Vale Royal Abbey Arms. Turn left here and continue in the direction of Frodsham for just over two miles to Hatchmere village. About 200 yards past the shop/cafe at the crossroads is the Carriers Inn and, opposite, a large car park and picnic area with toilets.
Public transport: BR to Chester, change for Delamere Station and join the route at the visitor centre 400 yards west. Trains from Chester run every 1-2 hours depending on the time of day.

The Carriers Inn, Hatchmere

This 300 year old lakeside pub got its name by being a popular place of refreshment for farmers carting their produce to the market at Ellesmere Port. Beers include cask-conditioned Burtonwood's bitter and mild. Opening hours are 11.30-15.00 and 6.00-23.00 Monday-

Saturday (in summer, Saturdays 11.30-23.00) and 12.00-15.00 and 19.00-10.30 on Sundays. The pub serves a good range of plain home-cooked meals (e.g. steak pie, gammon, lamb chops, vegetarian lasagne etc) at reasonable prices. Food is available 12.00-14.00 and 19.00-21.00 Monday-Saturday and 12.00-14.00 only on Sunday. Children are welcome in the beer garden but in the pub only for meals.

The Carriers Inn

Background

At around 2400 acres, the present Delamere Forest is a mere fraction of its size at the time of the Norman Conquest when it covered the whole area between the Weaver and the Gowy and extended as far south as Nantwich. The forest of Mara and Mondrem, as Delamere was then known, was a favourite hunting ground of the Earls of Chester but its main importance was as a source of oak for building timber. Delamere was also the lair of outlaws and after it was taken over by the crown as a royal forest in the 14th century the burghers of Chester petitioned Edward III to have it all cut down to remove their cover. However, by this time so much timber had already been extracted that Edward's son, the Black Prince, imposed strict measures to try to limit felling. Assarts – licensed clearances for farmland – also made large encroachments on the forest in the late Middle . Ages and by the 17th century so much of the tree cover had gone that the forest's once large population of deer had become extinct. By 1808 so few trees were left that Delamere was described as a 'heath affording a scanty subsistence to a few sheep and rabbits' rather than a forest.

This was the end of a gradual process of clearance that had been begun by Anglo-Saxon settlers long before the Norman Conquest, as is shown by the number of place-names in the area with the suffix 'ley' (from Old English 'leah': a clearing), e.g. Norley, 'the northern clearing'. The Anglo-Saxons also left their mark on the area in the shape of a fort on Eddisbury Hill, overlooking the present forest. The hill had first been fortified in the Iron Age c. 100 BC but the defences were levelled after the Roman conquest and the site was abandoned. The present ramparts were built in 914 on the orders of Aethelflaed the 'Lady of the Mercians' (a daughter of king Alfred) to protect the area against the Vikings who were beginning to settle on the Wirral at this time.

The birth of the modern Delamere forest came in 1812. The Napoleonic wars were at their height and massive warship building programmes had denuded the country's timber reserves so plans were set to reafforest the area. Early replanting was mainly of hardwoods and most of the forest's oak, beech and chestnut date from the 19th century. However, these did not flourish so the faster growing conifers which dominate the forest today were increasingly planted as the century progressed. With the increasing use of iron for shipbuilding, demand for oak was, in any case, falling while the demand for straight lengths of timber for pit-props was steadily growing. Many species of conifer were planted (the drab Sitka spruce was one of many which failed to flourish, fortunately) but the attractive Corsican pine was the most successful and this is the dominant tree in the forest today. Another major change came in 1867 when the construction of the Manchester-Chester railway line opened the forest to day trippers from the industrial towns to the north. The forest has been an important recreational area ever since.

Commercial exploitation of the forest was made more efficient after the Forestry Commission was set up in 1919, resulting in a drab and uniform forest. In recent years, however, the commission have adopted management policies which show greater sensitivity to conservation and recreational needs, creating a varied and attractive forest with trees of wide variety of ages. There are no deer these days but there is a healthy badger population, foxes are common and there is a varied bird life including, in winter, crossbills and gold-crests.

The survival of the forest, however modified, into the modern age has been greatly aided by its infertile, sandy soils. These sands were deposited by streams rushing from melting glaciers at the end of the Ice Age, some 12,000 years ago. As the glaciers retreated, isolated blocks of ice were frequently left buried in these deposits. When they melted a depression was formed, making a small lake. Delamere once had over 40 of these lakes and, indeed, gets its name from them: the 'forest of the meres'. Most of the lakes have silted up by natural processes, or been drained, but one of the survivors, Black Lake, is managed as a nature reserve. This charming place, more like a highland tarn than a lowland pond, is one of the highlights of this walk. The lake's main importance is that it has the largest breeding colony of whitefaced dragonflies in NW England but there is also a remarkable floating 'raft' of sphagnum moss on which grows the sundew, a carnivorous plant which catches small insects on its sticky leaves. Don't, under any circumstances, try walking on the raft to find these fascinating little plants – you will probably fall straight through it into the 15' deep water below. Given time, Black Lake will also silt up: as the sphagnum moss of the raft dies it falls to the bottom of the lake and will eventually fill it. The lake will first become a peat bog and, eventually, dry land.

The Walk

Walking for miles along forestry roads can get rather dull but don't expect that of this walk. For most of its length it skirts the edges of the forest giving a variety of scenery, from reedy lakes to mature pine and deciduous woodland and pastureland.

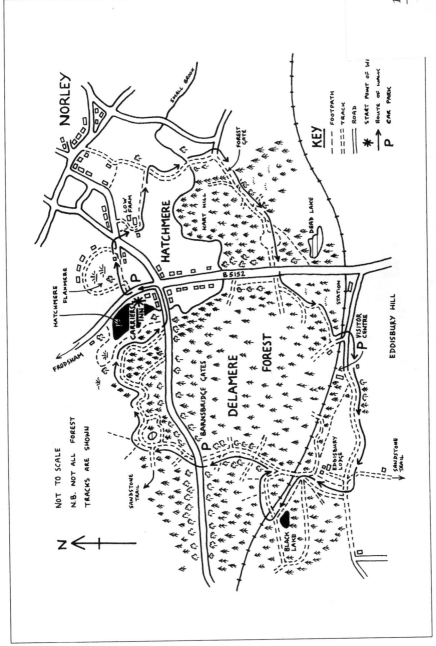

From Hatchmere, an attractive reedy lake surrounded by woods, take the unmade road which runs along the north edge of the picnic site and when, after about 150 yards, it bends sharp left continue straight on along the footpath which skirts Flaxmere, which is a marsh rather than a lake. A few hundred yards further on the path joins a lane which quickly brings you to the junction of School Lane and Post Office Lane. Follow Post Office Lane for about 25 yards and cross the stile on the right-hand side of the road. The right of way follows the hedge down to the farm track, passes between the two barns immediately ahead of you and turns sharp left round the back of a silage clamp (in winter this is the muddiest part of the walk – wear wellies!). Now walk along the hedge, crossing two awkward stiles, to reach a wide bridleway (the Delamere Way). Turn right and follow the clearly waymarked track over a hill with good views of the forest, through pasture and across a stream. About 200 yards beyond the stream, the bridleway ends at a gate. Turn right here, up a tree lined path, through a gate and into the forest.

The wide path sweeps downhill through pines, passing a yellow way marker, and then past mature beeches. Keep following the yellow way markers bearing right at post 22 into a clearing where the Forestry Commission sell Christmas trees in season. From here go straight across the B5152 and down a short descent. Keep left at marker post 14 and again at marker post 4 (the posts don't seem to follow any obvious numerical order). The sandiness of the forest soils is very apparent hereabouts and the extensive cleared area to the left has a distinctly heathland appearance. At marker post 3 the path meets an unsurfaced road, turn left, cross the railway bridge (which gives a good view of the ramparts of the Anglo-Saxon fort on Eddisbury Hill) and turn right. At the bottom of the hill is the forest visitor centre (with displays on forest management, shop and toilets: open 10.30-12.30 and 13.00-16.15 Monday-Friday and 10.30-16.45 Saturday and Sunday, admission free).

Leaving the visitor centre, continue along the track, which soon leaves the forest, and just past the entrance to Eddisbury Lodge turn right (signpost to Barnsbridge Gates) onto the Sandstone Trail and back into the forest. About 400 yards on, the footpath meets a forest road at post 20: go straight on for another 100 yards to an unnumbered post where three tracks branch off to your left. Ignore the first two and take the third which runs uphill at first and then parallel to a railway cutting. About 300 yards further on a stand of tall pines points out the position of Black Lake. If it is a warm summer day, sit down for a while and enjoy a free aerial display as dozens of dragonflies and damselflies dart over the lake like miniature helicopters.

From the lake, cross the railway bridge and stick to the main track as it loops around to rejoin the Sandstone Trail and then turn left, uphill. Between here and Barnsbridge Gates the route passes through mature deciduous woodland: mainly consisting of beech, oak and sweet chestnut. Go straight across the crossroads at post 49 and continue straight on to Barnsbridge Gates following the Sandstone Trail way markers. At the gates, cross the road to the forest track opposite and after about 25 yards bear right at post 48. Follow this track for about 300 yards until it turns sharp right. Head straight on here on the path past post 32 (where the Sandstone Trail branches off left) and around a swampy hollow which must once have been very similar to Black Lake. The track begins to pass through dense and gloomy pine plantations. At post 31 bear left and at the next major track junction (no numbered post at the time of writing) bear left again. This track loops round and reaches the switchback road after about half a mile, close to the edge of Hatchmere village. Turn left and walk down to the crossroads, then left again and so back to the Carriers Inn and the picnic area.

3. Around Little Budworth Common

Distance: Allow 3 hours for this 6½ mile walk

Maps: Landranger 1:50,000 – 117; Pathfinder 1:25,000 – 774 (SJ 46/56)

Map reference of start/finish: SJ 584663

How to get there

From Chester: Take the A51 as far as Tarvin, then the A54 as far as its junction with the A49 at a set of traffic lights. At the lights turn right for Whitchurch and after ¼ mile turn left just before you get to the garden centre (signpost Little Budworth and Oulton Park). After ½ mile turn left into Beech Road at a wooden car park sign. The car park is about 200 yards down, on the right.

From Wrexham: Take the A534 Nantwich road as far as its junction with the A49, where turn left for Warrington and after 4½ miles, at the traffic lights at the Red Fox, go straight on for Eaton (B5152). Go through Eaton and about ½ mile past the Red Lion pub turn right for Little Oulton Park/Winsford. At the crossroads go straight on past a small mere and past the main entrance to Oulton Park. Turn left into Coach Road opposite the ornamental archway, pass the first car park, and nearly a mile further on turn right into Beech Road (look out for the small wooden car park sign). The car park is about 200 yards down, on the right.

The Red Lion, Little Budworth

A friendly village pub. Opening hours are 11.00-15.00 and 18.00-23.00 Monday-Saturday and 12.00-15.00 and 19.00-22.30 on Sundays. Beers include cask conditioned Robinson's mild and bitter. The pub has a regular menu and daily specials: meals include, for example, turkey and ham pie, cod and prawn crumble, leek and mushroom crumble, liver and onions, steaks etc. Prices are about average. Food is served 11.00-14.00 and 18.00-21.00 Monday-Saturday and 12.00-14.00 and 19.00-21.00 on Sundays. There is a beer garden and the pub has a special family room. Ruth Ellis and her racing driver lover David Blakely often stayed at the Red Lion and the pub is regularly visited by big names from the racing world.

The Red Lion

The Alvanley Arms, Cotebrook

This attractive pub was originally built as a farmhouse in the 17th century. Opening hours are 11.30-15.00 and 17.30-23.00 Monday - saturday and 12.00-15.00 and 19.00-22.30 on Sundays. Beers include cask conditioned Robinson's bitter and mild and, in winter, Old Tom. Food is served 12.00-14.00 and 18.00-21.30 Wednesday-Saturday, 12.00-14.00 and 19.00-21.00 Sunday, 12.00-14.00 and 18.00-21.00 Monday-Tuesday. There is a set bar menu which includes steak pie, battered cod, chicken Italienne, chicken tikka, steaks etc and various vegetarian dishes such as chilli and hotpot. There are also daily specials, usually fresh seafood dishes and, in season, game. Prices are slightly above average. Children are welcome in the pub, though not in the bar itself. There is a beer garden with swings for children. Customers may leave their cars in the car park while they go for a walk but it is essential that they ask permission first.

Budworth Pool

Background

Little Budworth Common is, along with Delamere Forest, one of the few remnants of the great forest of Mara and Mondrem that covered most of west Cheshire in medieval times. At this time Little Budworth village was known as Budworth-le-Frith meaning 'Budworth in the woods' from an Old English word 'fyrhth' for woodland. The common was never cleared for agriculture because its sandy soils are almost sterile. Until this century the common was a heath but with the end of grazing birch trees have steadily encroached and it is mostly wooded now. In the 18th and 19th centuries the common was an important meeting place for Gipsies. Henrey Lovett, who claimed to be 'the King of the Gipsies', died here on 17th January 1744 aged 85 and is buried in Little Budworth churchyard. His grave can be found near the north-east corner of the church. The church itself is an odd mixture of an early 16th century tower and late Georgian nave and chancel: it is more attractive outside than in.

Much of the walk skirts the edges of Oulton Park which is now a motor racing circuit. Lovers of peace and quiet are well-advised to steer clear of this area when race meetings are in progress (most weekends from March to October: to check, ring the park office 01829-760301) as the squeals of tortured rubber and the howls of well-thrashed engines fill the air for miles around. Oulton was the seat of the Egertons, one the great landowning families of Cheshire, and saw a succession of halls. The last hall was built in 1720 after the old hall burned down and the park was landscaped at the same time. The new hall, in its turn, burned down in 1926, killing seven people and destroying a large collection of ancient manuscripts and works of art. The hall was not rebuilt and, after serving as a US army camp in World War II, the park was leased to the owners of Brands Hatch in 1952 who built the present circuit. Only an ornamental entrance survives of the hall's former glories.

The Walk

This is an easy walk along green lanes and, generally, easy to follow field paths. The going is mostly good, even after heavy rain, but a few sections get very muddy. There are also a few sections of road walking.

From the car park, return to Beech Road and turn left. At the junction with Coach Road, go straight across to the sandy bridlepath. Follow this for ¼ mile out of the woods and then between hedges through fields to a 'crossroads'. Go straight on for about 600 yards, past 'Hunter's Cottage' and where the track bends sharp right at a house take the path which goes straight on between the hedge and the edge of the garden (well-hidden signpost for Cotebrook). The path, which is narrow and gets churned up a bit by horses, begins to descend with high banks on either side and comes out on the A49 by telephone box.

Walk left down the road for a few yards to the cross roads. You could walk straight down the A49 here to the Alvanley Arms but I don't recommend it, the road is very busy and there is no footpath. Instead, cross over and walk up Utkinton Lane past the small 19th century church. Go straight across the next cross roads and carry on uphill past Hollins Hill Lane until you come to a stile signposted for

Cotebrook. You can see the pub from here across the field. Cross the field to the corner of the fence and follow the fence down to a stile by the A49. The stile is awkward because of a big drop down to the busy road on the far side. There is no footpath so watch out for traffic.

Cross the road to the pub and then go left down Eaton Lane for about ¼ mile, past one footpath sign by some houses and past the entrance to a water works, to a footpath sign and stile on the left by a holly tree. Unfortunately, Eaton Lane is moderately busy and there is no footpath. From the stile walk to the bottom of the bank and cross the field to a stile over a fence and immediately afterwards over another through a hedge and nettle bed. Now keep parallel to the left-hand hedge to a stile between two trees. Over the stile, turn right on a metalled lane for a short distance and where it bends right you will find two stiles on the left-hand side of the road.

Take the stile on the right-hand side of the gate and follow the field edge to a stile and footbridge. In the next field head straight for Moss Hall Farm, over a stile in a fence and then along the edge of a fence to reach the farm itself. Go round the right-hand side of the farm and onto a metalled lane which brings you to a T-junction opposite a post box in a whitewashed wall. Turn right down the road for a few yards and cross a stile by a gate on the left-hand side. Now cross two fields to come out on another lane after about 250 yards. Bear right and walk down the lane, which has wide grassy verges, and alongside the boundary wall of Oulton Park.

Just before you reach Parkwall Farm, near a prominent 'Beware Cattle Crossing' sign, cross a stile on the left and walk across the field to cross another stile right up against the park wall. For the next 600 yards or so the route goes through a succession of fields, keeping close to the wall all the way. Hard-up motor sport enthusiasts may be interested to know that the wall is ruinous and that the race-track can easily be seen from the path. At a dark, tree shadowed pond the wall turns sharply to the left. Cross the stile here (ignore the other stile almost facing you) and walk along the right-hand edge of the field towards Lower Farm. You leave the field over a footbridge over a small clear brook onto a metalled farm road. Turn left and

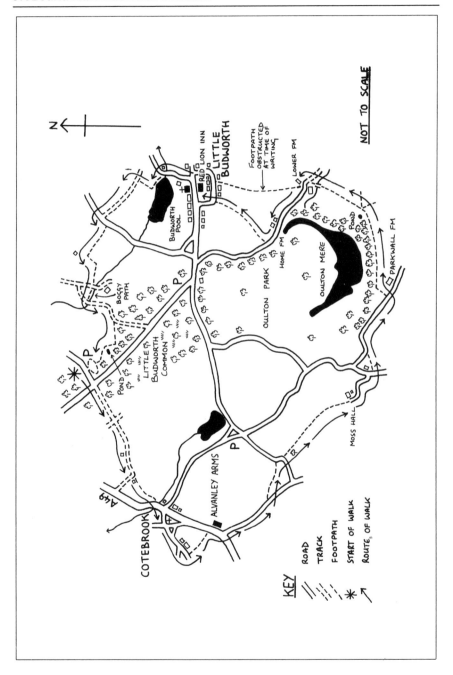

KEY

ROAD
TRACK
FOOTPATH
* START OF WALK
↗ ROUTE OF WALK

NOT TO SCALE

LITTLE BUDWORTH

RED LION INN

BUDWORTH POOL

FOOTPATH OBSTRUCTED AT TIME OF WRITING

LOWER FM

PARKWALL FM

POND

HOME FM

OULTON MERE

OULTON PARK

BOGGY PATH

LITTLE BUDWORTH COMMON

POND

MOSS HALL

ALVANLEY ARMS

COTEBROOK

A49

just past the farm buildings, where the road bears left, there is a gate into a field.

This is the start of a right of way which crosses the fields to Little Budworth. However, at the time of writing the gate had been chained up and nailed shut by the farmer at Lower Farm. Although you would be perfectly within your rights to climb over the fence and continue on your way, not everybody likes to risk a confrontation with an obstreperous farmer. So, if the obstruction has not been cleared by the time of publication, carry on down the lane for ¼ mile, past Home Farm, to a stile on the right by an oak tree. Cross the field in the direction of the tower of Little Budworth church which can be seen ahead, down a little valley, over a footbridge and up to the gate on the right-hand side of the hedge. Follow the side of the hedge through two fields to a road at the corner of a modern housing estate. Carry on straight ahead down the side of the estate to a T-junction and turn right for about 150 yards to reach the Red Lion opposite the parish church.

From the pub bear left around the outside of the churchyard into Mill Lane, past the Post Office/village shop and about 200 yards down the lane you come to the brook flowing out of Budworth Pool. The sandstone and brick house on the other bank of the brook was once a watermill and it is likely that there has been a watermill on this site since the Middle Ages as in the 14th century Budworth Pool was known as the *walkemulnepoul*, i.e. 'the watermill pool'. Just over the stream, on the left is a footpath (signpost Budworth Mere) which follows the reedy shore of the lake for 200 yards to a stile. The view over the lake to village, dominated by the church tower, is very attractive. The route leaves the lake shore almost at right angles and crosses two fields to a green lane. Turn left along the lane. For much of the way the lane is slightly sunken beneath banks covered with brambles, blackthorn and young elms.

After about 500 yards the green lane comes to a metalled road. Go left here for 25 yards or so and then over a stile on the right by a metal gate signposted to Whitehall Lane. Cross the field by heading just to the left of the white house with the red tiled roof to reach a stile through a hedge. In the next, small, field turn left and follow the hedge, then over another stile. In this field keep to the right of the line of telegraph poles until you can see a stile over a wooden fence at the bottom of a grassy bank. Cross this into a flowery, but marshy, hollow and over another stile onto a sandy track (a signpost here points back the way you've just come, to Park Road). Cross the stile almost immediately opposite and walk through a gloomy little wood along the bank of a shallow brook for about 50 yards to reach another sandy track. The path here is very muddy in most weathers and this section can be avoided by a short detour, going right up the track for 100 yards and then left for about the same distance to rejoin the route.

Turn left on the track, over the brook, and when, after about 400 yards, the road bends to the left turn right onto the path over the wooded common signposted to Coach Road. The path keeps within sight of the edge of the woods to the right. After 250 yards, the path divides: go right, then just past a sedgy woodland pool turn left onto a path which winds uphill at first, then crosses an area of heather and sandy heathland to come out at the Beech Road car park.

4. Bunbury and the Shropshire Union Canal

Distance: Allow 3½ hours for the 6 mile walk or 2½ for the 4 mile walk.

Maps: Landranger 1:50,000 – 117; Pathfinder 1:25,000 – 790 (SJ 45/55)

Map reference of start/finish: SJ 569581

How to get there

From Chester: Take the A51(T) to its junction with the A49(T) at Tarporley, then follow the A49 in the direction of Whitchurch. After passing the ornate Wild Boar Hotel, about 3 miles on, take the second turning on the left (signposted to Bunbury) and turn left again in the village centre to reach the Dysart Arms about ¼ mile further on. Park in the small car park by the cemetery on the north side of the parish church or around the green to its east.

Public Transport: Huxley's Travel service C83 run one service a day between Chester and Bunbury (Mon-Sat) but is geared more for travel into Chester than out of it.

From Wrexham: Take the A534 to its junction with the A49(T), then turn left in the direction of Warrington for 1½ miles and just after the Red Rum Inn turn right on the road signposted to Haughton. Turn left at the Crewe Arms and go straight on through the village for nearly a mile until you reach the Dysart Arms opposite the parish church. Park in the small car park by the cemetery on the north side of the church or around the green to its east.

The Dysart Arms, Bunbury

This attractive brick-built pub was originally built as a farmhouse about 300 years ago and still has an original inglenook fireplace in the lounge. It was converted into a pub in the 19th century. Beers include cask conditioned Thwaites and Tetley bitter. Opening hours 12.00-15.30 and 17.30-23.00 Monday-Friday, 12.00-23.00 Saturday and 12.00-15.00 and 19.00-22.30 on Sundays. The pub serves meals from the basic sausage and chips to a variety of casseroles and vegetarian meals. Food is served 12.00-14.30 and 18.00-21.30 Monday-Saturday and 12.00-14.30 and 19.00-21.30 on Sundays. Children are welcome in the beer garden and in the pub at lunchtimes for meals. Walkers using the pub may leave their cars in the car park.

The Dysart Arms

The Davenport Arms, Calveley

An unfussy pub on the A51(T), popular with canal boaters. Beers include cask conditioned Burtonwood mild and bitter, Bass and Worthington Best Bitter. Opening hours 11.00-23.00 Monday-Saturday, 12.00-15.00 and 19.00-22.30 Sunday. The pub serves a wide range of home-cooked meals including pies, curries, steaks and vegetarian meals at good value prices: available all day (the pub also does breakfasts). Children are welcome in the pub and there is a play area in the beer garden. Dogs are allowed in the pub. Walkers using the pub may leave their cars in the car park.

The Beeston Castle Hotel, Beeston

This large pub was built in 1846 by Lord Tollemache (who also built nearby Peckforton Castle) as a station hostelry for the newly constructed Crewe and Chester Railway. Beeston's twice weekly cattle market was originally held in the pub's back yard. Beers available include cask conditioned Bass and a wide variety of guest beers. Opening hours are 11.00-15.00 and 17.30-23.00 Monday, Tuesday and Thursday, 11.00-23.00 Wednesday, Friday and Saturday and 12.00-15.00 and 19.00-22.30 on Sundays. Meals are served in the bar and in the restaurant from an extensive and varied menu which includes special children's meals. Food is available 11.00-14.00 and 18.30-21.30 Monday-Saturday (bar snacks only on Tuesday night) and on Sunday from 12.00-14.00 and 19.00-21.30. Children are welcome in the beer garden and in the pub for meals at lunchtime and in the evening until 22.00. Dogs are allowed in the public bar. Except on market days (Wednesdays and Fridays) when the pub is very busy, walkers using the pub may leave their cars in the car park but please ask first.

Background to Walk

Bunbury is really an amalgamation of two villages. Higher Bunbury nestles around the parish church on a hilltop and dates back to Anglo-Saxon times. Lower Bunbury, about ¼ mile away, began to grow up in Tudor times but is now the centre of the village. Further expansion took place to the west of Lower Bunbury in the 19th century after the enclosure of Bunbury Heath.

Bunbury's glory is its church, one of the finest in Cheshire. The church was founded in the eighth century but the church has been rebuilt many times in its long history; most recently in 1950 as a result of a near miss by a stray German bomb in 1940. The oldest surviving stonework dates to 1320 but most of the present church was built in 1385-6 with endowments from Sir Hugh de Calveley whose mighty effigy dominates the chancel. Calveley, who was reputed to have been about 7' tall, was a companion of the Black Prince and one of the great captains of the English armies in the Hundred Years War: he was still campaigning in Spain in 1388 when

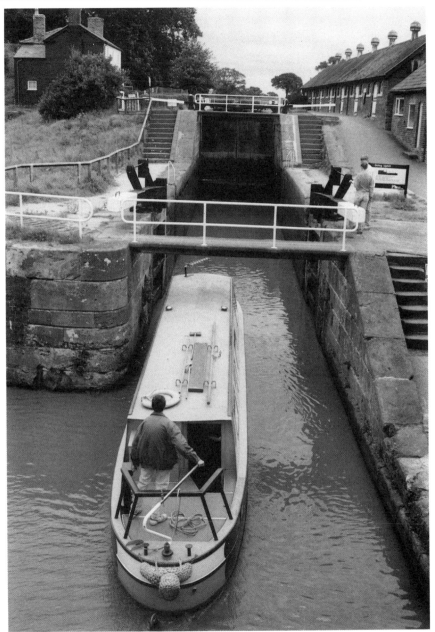

Tilston Lock on the Shropshire Union Canal

he was in his seventies. Medieval man was painfully aware of the consequences of sin and, as a professional soldier, Calveley would unavoidably have sinned more than most. By rebuilding his parish church, Calveley will have hoped to have made his peace with God. Close to the altar is the effigy of another long-lived warrior, Sir George Beeston. Born in 1499 he fought in a succession of French and Scottish wars before becoming an admiral and commanding the Royal Navy's first HMS Dreadnought against the Armada in 1588, aged 89! He died in 1601, having been an eyewitness to most of the Tudor age.

A quarter of a mile east of the church is Bunbury Mill, the first of about a dozen flour mills which once were powered by the river Gowy. There was a timber-framed mill on this site in the 17th century but this had probably burned down by 1839. In 1850 a new brick-built mill was built on the site using the old stone foundations. The rebuilding was a tribute to the self-sufficiency of nineteenth-century rural communities. The walls were built of locally made bricks and local elm trees provided the floor beams and the wooden buckets of the mill wheel. The mill's 260 beechwood gear cogs were hand carved by local millwrights and most of the iron screws, nuts and bolts were forged and threaded by the local blacksmith. The only important part of the mill which had to be brought from outside were the millstones, which came from Birmingham: the local sandstone is not hard-wearing enough to make good millstones. The new mill was worked continuously, producing fine flour and animal meal, until a flood breached the mill dam in 1960, causing the mill to be abandoned. The site passed into the hands of North West Water in 1974 who restored the mill in 1976-7 with the advice of its last miller Tom Parker who had worked the mill from 1924 to the night of the flood in 1960. A sign on the mill's door recalls the old conviction of country folk, no doubt justified in many cases, that millers regularly cheated their customers by stealing more of the flour than was due to them: 'Remember milner be kiend unto the poor and of the rich take but thy deu beshoor'. The mill is now open to the public at weekends and Bank Holidays between Easter and 30th September (admission charge).

The canal came to Bunbury in 1772. At first it simply linked

Nantwich to the Dee at Chester but in 1797 it was extended to link Ellesmere in Shropshire to the Mersey at Netherpool (now known as Ellesmere Port). In 1829 Telford incorporated the canal into the Shropshire Union canal linking Wolverhampton to the sea. There is much of interest to see along the canal, not least the staircase lock at Bunbury, which has two chambers. At the top of the lock is a boat-shed which was formerly a stable for the horses which towed the 'Flyboats' – 'express' canal boats. These ran to a timetable between Wolverhampton and Ellesmere Port and the horses were changed every 20 miles to keep speeds up. At Tilston and Beeston Stone Locks look out for the small whitewashed round buildings by the towpath. These were lengthsman's huts, where the canal's equivalent of the railway linesman kept tools and could shelter in bad weather. They had a fireplace inside and were probably quite cosy. The last lock on the walk, Beeston Iron Lock is just that. Unstable glacial sands had caused problems with the lock here since the canal was first built so, in 1828, Telford solved the problem by building a cast iron tank to hold the lock chamber.

The Walk

This is an easy walk through pastureland and includes an attractive stretch of canal towpath.

If you are doing the **shorter version** of the walk, take the path which heads north along the east side of the new cemetery opposite the church. A few hundred yards brings you onto a lane. Turn right and another ¼ mile brings you to a cross roads; go straight across to join the canal towpath at Tilston Lock ½ mile further on.

To start the longer walk, cross to the far side of the green on the east side of the parish church where you will find a stile. Go straight across the field and over another stile to reach the car park for Bunbury Mill. Turn left to rejoin the lane, then turn right and follow the lane for about 400 yards to a gravel drive. About 25 yards up the drive cross the stile on the left-hand side and go straight across the field to a gate onto another metalled lane. Turn right and follow the lane to where it makes a sharp turn to the right. Cross the stile on the left into a large field and strike a diagonal line across it. You won't be able to see the way out so look for a tall ash tree and aim for this – there is a stile just on the other side of it. In the next field turn right and follow the hedge to another stile; cross it, then walk in the direction of the gate by a solitary oak tree. The stile is actually tucked away in the corner of the hedge to the left of the tree. To cross the next field aim to the left of both Clays Farm and the line of telegraph poles which crosses the field. Cross the small footbridge into another small field and strike across at an angle of about 45° to find a stile in the hedge. Once over it you will find yourself on the towpath of the Shropshire Union Canal.

If you want to visit the Davenport Arms, turn right and cross over the canal bridge: the pub is 200 yards away at the end of the unsurfaced lane. Retrace your steps to rejoin the route. Otherwise, turn left. There are no route finding difficulties for the next 2½ miles of easy walking along the towpath The little river Gowy keeps the canal company on the left all the way along this section of the towpath and by the time Bunbury Locks have been passed it has grown large enough to have cut itself a steep-sided little valley. At Tilston Locks look out for the first of the two lengthsman's huts. Shortly after Tilston Locks the valley opens out and you get a good view of Beeston Castle perched on its craggy hill. In summer, the banks of this section of towpath are rich in wildflowers, including masses of delightfully scented meadowsweet. Carry on past Beeston Stone Lock, where there is another lengthsman's hut (a small kiosk here sells soft drinks, ice cream etc from Easter to late October) to Beeston Iron Lock and at bridge 107 leave the canal.

Go under the railway bridge and through the main entrance to the cattle market. The market is held every Wednesday and Friday and is a thriving concern with livestock auctions and stalls selling everything from the ubiquitous green wellies and Barbours to toilet rolls. Walk right to the top of the market yard, across a small paddock and onto a path which is confined to the field edge by a wire fence. The path leaves the field up a short steep bank and at the top a superb view of Beeston Castle and its Victorian neighbour Peckforton Castle suddenly appears. A few yards further on the path meets a tarmac drive: turn left and walk up to the lane. Take the footpath immediately opposite (signposted to Spurstow and Bunbury). Cross the

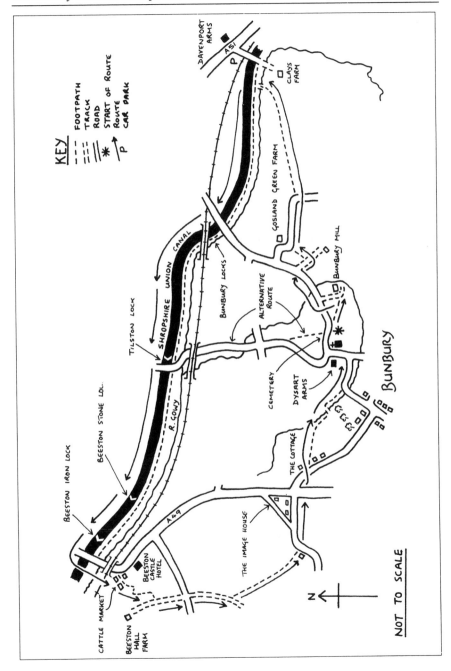

second stile into a large field and cross it to the next stile which can just be seen where the hedge ends and is replaced by a wire fence. Continue in roughly the same line across the next field (aim between the third and fourth telegraph poles, counting from the right-hand corner of the field) to another stile. Once over this, aim to the left of the grey house, through a small field and onto a lane. Turn left and walk straight on down along the lane to the A49.

A short detour here will take you to the curious Image House, a 19th century cottage decorated with rustic carvings. They are probably just a piece of whimsy but there are local stories associating them with a poacher who was sentenced to transportation. On his return he decorated his house with images of his enemies, perhaps in the belief that the images had some magical power to harm them. The house will be found 250 yards north on the left-hand side of the A49.

Cross the main road and walk down the lane signposted to Bunbury and take the drive (public footpath sign) on the left just past 'The Cottage'. The drive turns into a cobbled path which leads into a small field and almost immediately over another into a larger field. Cross this by aiming to the right of the solitary oak at the top of the low hill. At the top of this hill you get a lovely view of Bunbury, dominated by the church tower, nestling among trees in the folds of this gently rolling pastureland. Go straight across the next field in the direction of the end of the wood, then follow the hedge through the next field to a footbridge over another river Gowy (the confusion is ended near Tilston Locks where the two rival Gowys join up). The last few hundred yards of the walk are through a shallow valley with the infant river on your right and Bunbury sitting on top of the hill to your left. When you reach the lane, turn left and walk the short distance uphill to the Church and the Dysart Arms.

5. The Peckforton Hills and Beeston Castle

Distance: Allow 2½ hours for this 4½ mile walk

Maps: Landranger 1:50,000 – 117; Pathfinder 1:25,000 – 790 (SJ 45/55)

Map reference of start/finish: SJ 524566

How to get there

From Chester: Take the A41(T) south for about 4 miles and turn off for Tattenhall. In Tattenhall, turn left at the Letters Inn (signposts for Burwardsley and candle workshops). At Burwardsley, turn left at the post office, where there is a wooden sign for the Pheasant Inn, and drive up the hill until you come to a telephone box at a cross-roads. The Pheasant is just down the lane to the left. There is no public off-road parking in Higher Burwardsley.

Public transport: Service 64 (Mon-Sat) from Chester goes to both Burwardsley and Beeston village. The nearest the bus goes to the start of the walk is Burwardsley Post Office, about ¾ mile from the Pheasant Inn in Higher Burwardsley, so walkers may prefer to start the walk from Beeston Village instead.

From Wrexham: Take the A534 as far as the Coppermines Inn at Brown Knowl and turn left (signpost Harthill, Burwardsley and candle workshops). Just out of Harthill, turn right and right again a mile further on. After about 150 yards the road divides: bear left past the church and when you come to T-junction turn right uphill until you come to a telephone box at a cross-roads. The Pheasant is just down the lane to the left. There is no public off-road parking in Higher Burwardsley.

The Pheasant, Higher Burwardsley

This is a characterful 17th century inn with excellent views to the west. Opening hours are 12.00-15.00 and 19.00-23.00 Monday-Saturday and 12.00-15.00 (also 15.00-17.00 for teas) and 19.00-22.30 on Sundays. Beers include cask conditioned Bass and Worthington's bitter. The pub has a well-deserved reputation for good food, though the quality is reflected in above average prices. Food is available 12.00-14.15 and 19.00-21.00 seven days. There is a beer garden and children's play area and children are welcome in the conservatory (up to 20.00) but not in the pub itself. Walkers using the pub may leave their cars in the car park but should ask the landlord first (the car park may be locked when the pub is closed).

The Pheasant

Background

This walk is dominated by two hilltop fortresses, Beeston Castle and Peckforton Castle. Beeston Castle owes much of its grandeur to its superb position atop an isolated craggy hill which gives command-ing views over the Cheshire plain. The hill itself has seen human occupation from prehistoric times – recent excavations have un-earthed Neolithic flint arrowheads, a Bronze Age axehead and an Iron Age hill fort. The castle was begun in 1225 by Ranulf, sixth earl of Chester (1170-1232), as a 'state of the art' fortress incorporating all of the latest developments in military architecture including wall towers and gate-houses. Ranulf had been a crusader and it is likely that Beeston's design has been influenced by the formidable crusader castles of the Holy Land. The castle basically consists of two fortified enclosures or 'baileys'. The outer bailey contained workshops and stables. The inner bailey acted much like the keep of a Norman castle. Perched on top of the hill and protected by cliffs on one side and a rock cut ditch on the others, it could have been easily defended by a determined and alert garrison.

In his younger days Ranulf had been an enthusiastic leader of raids into Wales but in 1218 he agreed an alliance with Llewellyn the Great, prince of Gwynedd, which brought peace to the borderlands for many years. Beeston Castle, then, was probably not built to intimidate the Welsh. The earl was not on close terms with the English king Henry III and it is likely that the new castle was mainly intended to impress the king with Ranulf's power and wealth.

The castle was acquired by the crown in 1237 and during the reign of Edward I (1272-1307) Beeston was an important base for campaigns in Wales. Thereafter it declined in importance and decay set in. During the Civil War the castle was hastily brought back into commission and garrisoned by Parliament. But in 1643 a force of nine Royalist soldiers climbed the cliffs on the north side of the castle, taking the 60 strong garrison by surprise and forcing it to surrender. The unfortunate Parliamentary commander, Captain Thomas Steele, was later court-marshalled and shot for his failure to hold the castle. Parliament eventually retook the castle in 1646 after an 11 month siege. After the war some of the defences were destroyed and the rest left to decay. One legend associated with the castle is that Richard II hid part of his treasure in the well in 1399. Sadly, thorough excavations have revealed nothing.

Peckforton Castle looks from a distance every inch a medieval fortress, strong enough to be a rival to Beeston only three-quarters of a mile away. It is, however, an impostor, built by Lord Tollemache between 1844 and 1851 as a luxury home, and is a marvellous example of Victorian romantic medievalism. Unlike most Victorian mock castles, Peckforton makes few visible concessions to comfort and even close up it looks fully capable of withstanding a siege. It is such a convincing impostor that the leading Victorian architect

Gilbert Scott described Peckforton as 'the very height of masquerading'.

Both castles are open to the public: Beeston all year, Peckforton only from Easter to mid September.

The walk starts in the village of Burwardsley, a rather dispersed community on the western slopes of the Peckforton Hills. The village is first recorded in the twelfth century as 'Berewardesleya'. The name probably comes from Burgweard's leah meaning Burgweard's glade – the area was still thickly forested at that time. Burwardsley did not become recognised as a community in its own right until 1735 when it became a separate parish. Before this it had been treated as an outlying part of Bunbury. Burwardsley is probably best known today for its candle-making workshops which attract a great many visitors on summer weekends.

17th century cottages at Beeston

The other village visited on the walk is Beeston. Medieval documents record the village's name as Buistone, so the village probably gets its name from the craggy hill which is now occupied by the castle. What the first element of the name means is uncertain but it may have Celtic roots. The part of the Beeston visited on this walk is the original centre of the village. However, when the canal and, later, the railway were built in the early nineteenth century, the commercial centre of the village shifted north-east to the area of the cattle market on the A49.

The Walk

Start by walking down the metalled lane past the Pheasant Inn (don't bother driving down here – there's nowhere to park) and follow it for nearly ½ mile until it ends by Spring House Farm at a white gate plastered with notices (the owners of the Peckforton estate just love notices). Go through the gate and onto a track surfaced with alien-looking limestone chippings. After about 300 yards the Sandstone Trail joins the track from the right. There are good views out to the west here but they will soon be obscured by a growing pine plantation. The track continues easily on its way very gently descending, sometimes between mossy banks, with oak woods on the steep slopes to the right and fields and pine plantations to the left.

About a mile from Spring House Farm, the track comes out the woods onto a metalled lane. Beeston Castle on its craggy hill dominates the view to the north. Turn right and continue down the lane to Moathouse Farm (N.B. the right of way shown on current editions of the Ordnance Survey 50,000 and 25,000 maps leaving Moathouse Farm in the direction of Beeston Castle no longer exists: it has been replaced by a new right of way which leaves the lane 300 yards to the east).

Continue on the lane for another 300 yards past Moathouse Farm to a stile and Sandstone Trail signpost on the left-hand side of the lane. Follow the trail along the edge of the field, across a footbridge over a small brook and then through another field to come out on the lane by 'Tabernacle Cottage'. Spare a backward glance here to Peckforton Castle, which looks impressive from this angle, before crossing the lane to a stile (signpost to Beacon Hill). Climb up through a dense and gloomy pinewood and then bear right alongside a stone wall to come out at a car park and picnic area near the entrance to Beeston Castle. A small snack bar here is open for most of the year.

From the car park turn right and then left at the T-junction into the small village of Beeston. Bear left again at a rather scruffy garage with two roofs, one above the other – presumably the lower one leaks – and a few hundred yards further on take the right turn, signposted to Bunbury. Walk past Brook Farm and an attractive 17th century cruck-framed cottage and where the road bends sharp left take the track on the right signposted to Peckforton. This joins a very mucky farm track after a few yards and almost opposite is a stile into a huge park-like field, dotted with mature trees and overlooked by the towers of Peckforton Castle on its wooded hill. Cross this field to the pine wood on the far side. The stile into the wood is not easy to see until you get quite close: to find it, keep within about 100 yards of the left-hand edge of the field and when you reach a flooded marl pit the stile can be seen by a gate with a few larches on either side. You are soon through the wood and out the other side into another vast pasture. Immediately ahead can be seen the table-topped hill of Stanner Nab and below it the turretted gatehouse to the grounds of Peckforton Castle. Head straight for the gatehouse and you will come to a stile tucked away right in the corner of the field which you cross to a metalled lane.

Turn left and follow the lane for about a ¼ mile to a set of stone steps on the right-hand side of the lane leading up to a stile and signpost to Burwardsley. Now cross a series of four stiles as the path climbs gradually across the side of the hill to reach a line of sycamore and beech trees. Turn right under these trees for a few yards until you come to a track surfaced with limestone chippings. Go left here onto a roughly cobbled track and turn right, uphill. The gradient eases soon after the track passes under a stone bridge, built to carry a tramway for transporting stone from nearby quarries for the construction of Peckforton Castle. The cobbles end soon after the bridge too and the track is surfaced with ash, chippings or some-times runs over bedrock. Carry straight on this track, through young plantations, and at a brick cottage the track becomes a metalled lane which takes you quite steeply down to the telephone box in Higher Burwardsley and the start of the walk.

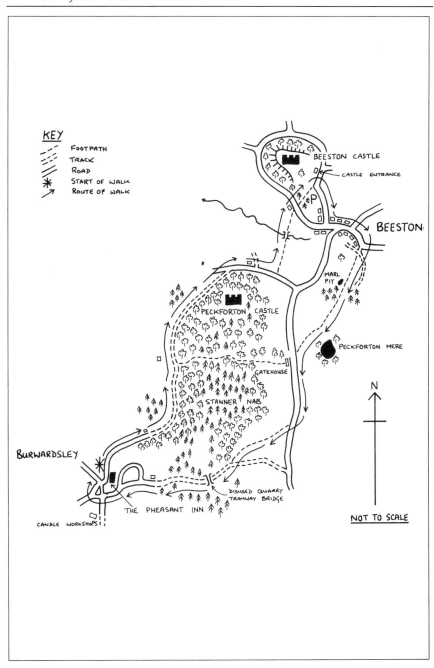

6. Rawhead and Maiden Castle

Distance: Allow at least 3 hours for this 5½ mile walk

Maps: Landranger 1:50,000 – 117; Pathfinder 1:25,000 – 790 (SJ 45/55)

Map reference of start/finish: SJ 500543

How to get there

From Chester: Leave Chester on the A41. Then at the roundabout at Broxton turn onto the A534. The Copper Mines Inn is two miles further on (¾ mile past the Durham Heifer). There is a small amount of roadside parking on the left just before you get to the pub.

Public transport: Services 64, C59 and C65 from Chester to Brown Knowl (are quite frequent, Mon-Fri).

From Wrexham: Leave Wrexham on the A534, Nantwich road. The Copper Mines Inn is on the right about 2 miles past the picnic area by the roundabout at Broxton (about ¾ mile past the Durham Heifer). There is limited roadside parking on the left just before you get to the pub.

The Copper Mines Inn, Brown Knowl

A very food-orientated pub which is used to catering for walkers. Opening hours 12.00-15.00 and 19.00-23.00 Monday to Saturday (late July and August the pub opens an hour earlier in the evening) and 12.00-15.00 and 19.00-22.30 Sundays. Beers include cask conditioned Burtonwood's bitter and Bass. There is an extensive menu of snacks and full meals ranging from seafood and steaks to Indian, Italian and vegetarian options. Food is available 12.00-14.30 and 19.00-21.30 Tuesday to Saturday and 12.00-14.30 and 19.00-21.00 Sundays and Mondays. There is a large beer garden but well-behaved children are welcome in the pub at any time. Walkers using the pub are welcome to leave their cars in the pub's large car park.

The Copper Mines Inn

Background

Raw Head gets its name from its bright red sandstone cliffs. These have been quarried in the past for their very fine sand which was prized as a scouring powder. A number of caves have been left behind by these activities and this walk passes close to at least four of them – the Queen's Parlour, Bloody Bones Cave, Musket's Hole and Mad Allen's Hole – though only the second is easy to find. Despite their mundane origins some of these caves have interesting folk tales associated with them. Bloody Bones Cave, on the very summit of Raw Head is reputed to have been the hide-out of a gang of outlaws. A little further to the south and lower down the escarpment is Musket's Hole and this really was inhabited as it contains a stone sleeping shelf, chimney and wall sockets for beams. Mad Allen's Hole, on Bickerton Hill, is a large cave with two levels. Who its eponymous occupant was is not known but he has been associated with John Harris of Handley who is said to have become a recluse living in caves for 70 years after his parents stopped him marrying his true love.

Copper was mined intermittently at Gallantry Bank from 1690 to 1929. The deposits were not very rich and it seems that the mines were only worked when the price of copper was high. The shafts were sealed after the mine closed and the buildings demolished: all that remains is the red sandstone pumphouse chimney which dates from 1856.

Gallantry Bank is a corruption of Gallows-tree Bank, so called, it is said, because the body of a murderer named Holford was hung in chains here in 1640. Five years later the place was the scene of the mass execution of 12 Parliamentarian prisoners-of-war by that dashing cavalier prince Rupert who hanged them from a crab-apple tree: perhaps it was this rather than Holford's gibbet that was the gallows tree?

The earliest evidence of human activity on these hills is Maiden Castle, an Iron Age hillfort on Larkton Hill. The fort was protected by cliffs on its north-west side and on the south-east by a double rampart and ditch system. The ramparts, which are best preserved at the southern perimeter of the fort, were built of earth with a facing

The hamlet of Harthill and its 17th-century church

of stone and were strengthened with a timber framework. When built, the ramparts would have been about 12' high. The fort had only one entrance, on the north, about 40 yards from the cliff edge. The ramparts here turn inwards to create a narrow passageway about 50 ft long with a gate and sentry post at the end. Recent radiocarbon dating of material from the ramparts has shown that the fort was burned in c. 400 BC, perhaps as the result of an attack.

Bickerton Hill and Larkton Hill have between them the largest area of heathland in Cheshire but birch scrub has been slowly taking the heath over since grazing was stopped in 1930. To help preserve the heath, the National Trust grazes Welsh Black cattle, which eat the birch saplings, on the hills between February and July. Welsh Black cattle are an appropriate choice for this site, like the fort, their origins go back to before the Roman conquest.

The Walk

For the most part this walk is on well-drained, often sandy, paths but there is a lot of up and down involved.

From the Coppermines Inn, walk west along the main road (there is a pavement) and just past the first farm on the right take the path signposted to Harthill and Burwardsley. Stick to the field edge, then turn left in the next field and right in the one after that. Follow the field boundary (first a hedge and then a fence) uphill to the corner of the pinewood on the hill top and walk along its edge to Church Farm and so to Harthill. Harthill has a pleasing early 17th century church, a green, sandstone houses and school and an excellent position on a shoulder of the Peckforton Hills giving good views: it ought to be an attractive little hamlet but it has a slightly neglected air about it.

Walk down the side of the green, cross the road and go down Garden Lane (signposted to Rawhead and Burwardsley). This becomes a grassy path, which can be a bit overgrown in summer, which leads into a field. Walk straight up the hill, keeping to the edge of the field until you come to a stile into the pines and beeches of Bodnick Wood. The path levels out in the wood and leads out into a steeply sloping field by a cottage. The view ahead is now dominated by the thickly wooded escarpment of Raw Head. Cross the top of the field to a track, then walk straight across through beech trees to reach a metalled lane after a short steep ascent. At the lane turn left and walk uphill until you can see it bend to the right. Here take the path on the right, signposted to Bickerton and Burwardsley. The path gains height steadily (the very steep path which branches off to the left leads to the Queens Parlour) through dense pine, ash and birch wood to reach the Sandstone Trail on the very edge of the escarpment. Turn right and a few hundred yards further on you will reach the trig point on the rocky summit of Raw Head.

The views west and south are tremendous on a clear day. The towers of Liverpool's two cathedrals are surprisingly prominent on the north-western horizon, while the whole length of the Clwydian Hills can be seen, with the Berwyn Mountains overtopping them to the south-west. To the south The Wrekin and the south Shropshire hills are prominent as are the Breidden Hills near Welshpool. The cave just below the summit is Bloody Bones Cave, reputed once to have been the lair of outlaws.

For the next 2½ miles the walk follows the Sandstone Trail and there are few route-finding problems. From the summit the trail follows the edge of the escarpment SW gradually descending to Gallantry Bank on the A534. There are excellent views all the way as the path skirts the tops of brightly coloured crags which make a sharp contrast with the greens of the surrounding woodland. After about ¾ mile the path passes some pheasant breeding pens and leads onto an unsurfaced lane at Chiflik Farm. A little over 100 yards down this track you will come to a signpost for the copper mines. There is little to see but a detour, retracing your steps afterwards, will not take long. Otherwise, continue down the track to the main road. Now known prosaically as the A534, in the Middle Ages this road was called the 'Walesmonsway' and was the main route to Wales for Cheshire salt traders.

Cross the road and take the lane opposite signposted for Bickerton, Cholmondley etc. Go straight down the lane and over the crossroads to Bickerton church. This appealingly simple small

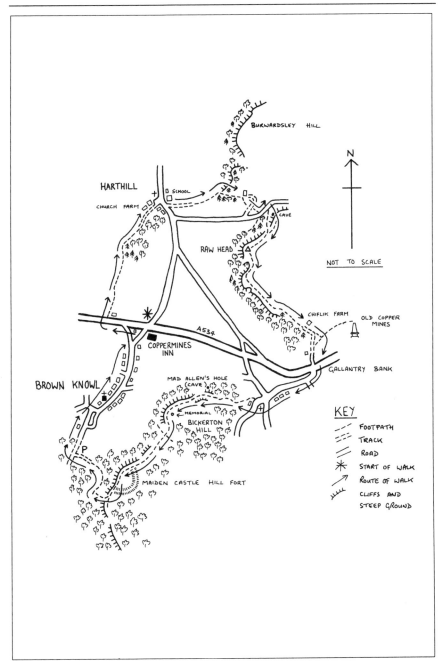

BURWARDSLEY HILL

N

HARTHILL

☐ SCHOOL

CHURCH FARM

CAVE

RAW HEAD

NOT TO SCALE

CHIFLIK FARM

OLD COPPER MINES

A534

COPPERMINES INN

GALLANTRY BANK

BROWN KNOWL

MAD ALLEN'S HOLE (CAVE)

MEMORIAL

BICKERTON HILL

P

MAIDEN CASTLE HILL FORT

KEY

- - - FOOTPATH

=== TRACK

═══ ROAD

✳ START OF WALK

↗ ROUTE OF WALK

CLIFFS AND STEEP GROUND

church was built in 1840 by public subscription: before this Bickerton had been part of the parish of Malpas and the local parishioners had to make a 10 mile round trip to attend church on Sundays. A few yards up the lane from the church, the Sandstone Trail branches off on the right, through a kissing gate and into the dense birch woods of Bickerton Hill. After going through a second kissing gate, the path begins to climb more steeply before levelling out. Shortly after the path reaches the foot of a line of low sandstone cliffs.

At this point you can detour off the route to find Mad Allen's Hole. Immediately before the path reaches these low cliffs, scramble down the steep, overgrown, slope on the right: if you can't fly, don't cut off the path before you can see the cliffs as there is a well-hidden line of cliffs below the path. As you descend, bear right to reach the base of this line of cliffs. Follow the cliffs along, passing one small cave, to reach an area of massive fallen boulders: Mad Allen's Hole is behind them at the base of the cliff. The cave is best looked for in the winter when the bracken and brambles have died down.

The main route continues, almost on the level and soon after passing the row of low cliffs the path emerges onto open heathland of bilberry and heather by a memorial to Kitty Wheeldon, from where you can see the final summit of the day, Larkton Hill. The path now descends a little before climbing again onto Larkton Hill. Keep following the Sandstone Trail signs and ignore the rather enigmatic symbols which appear from time to time on short marker posts (actually new waymarked walks laid out by the National Trust). On the summit of Larkton Hill are the ramparts of an Iron Age fort, Maiden Castle. Just outside the southern ramparts is a small memorial plaque, take the downhill path on your right here. The path becomes steep, crossing an easy step, before reaching a level 'col' where four paths meet. Take the right-hand path and continue downhill: clearings around here give good views of the cliffs which protected the west side of Maiden castle. These woods are criss-crossed with paths but the route keeps always to the widest one, eventually going through a gate and past a small playing field to a car parking area. Turn right down the sandy track and through the metal gate onto the lane at 'Tanglewood'. Follow the lane down to a 'T' junction, turn right and walk through the village of Brown Knowl. As you pass the brick Methodist church you can see the grave of John Wedgwood, of the famous pottery family, who died in 1869 – it has, appropriately, got an urn on top of a pillar. Keep left past the telephone box at the corner of Reading Room Lane and at the next junction turn right to finish the walk at the pub about 200 yards further on.

7. Hills and meres around Marbury

Distance: Allow at least 2½ hours for this 5½ mile walk

Maps: Landranger 1:50,000 – 117 Pathfinder 1:25,000 – 807 (SJ 44/54)

Map reference of start/finish: 539464

How to get there

From Chester: Take A41(T) as far as No Man's Heath and turn left on the lane for Bickley. Ignore the first right turning but thereafter bear right at every junction until you reach the A49 at Bickley. Turn right here in the direction of Whitchurch and after ½ a mile turn left onto the lane signposted for Marbury. At first bear right at every road junction but at the first junction after crossing the canal bear left into Marbury village.

From Wrexham: Follow the A525 to Whitchurch. At the roundabout on the by-pass west of Whitchurch turn left in the direction of Warrington on the A41 and at the next roundabout turn right into Whitchurch. After nearly a mile you will come to another roundabout: turn right here and then bear left at the mini-roundabout immediately afterwards. About 300 yards further on turn left on the road signposted to Deermoss Hospital and Marbury. Keep on this road, past a left turn signposted to Wirswall. Then, after about 1½ miles, bear left at a road junction and left again ¾ mile further on into Marbury village.

The Swan Inn, Marbury

Attractively situated by the village green, this pub was built in 1885 to replace an 18th century inn. The pub once provided a communal bakehouse for the village. Opening hours are 12.00-15.00 and 19.00-23.00 Monday-Saturday and 12.00-15.00 and 19.00-22.30 Sundays. Beers include cask conditioned Greenall's bitter and Stone's bitter. Food is available 12.00-14.00 and 19.00-21.00 seven days. There is a regular menu of snacks and main meals (toasties to steaks) as well as daily specials and vegetarian meals. Children are welcome in the pub and there is a special Children's menu. There is a beer garden. The pub has a large car park where walkers using the pub may leave their cars.

The Swan Inn

The Willeymoor Lock Tavern, Whitchurch

This canalside pub was built at the end of the 18th century as a lock keeper's cottage and stables. Opening hours 12.00-15.00 (14.00 in winter) and 18.0023.00 Monday-Saturday and 12.00-15,00 and 19.00-22.30 on Sundays. Beers include cask conditioned Theakston's bitter and two guest beers, There is a large beer garden and play area but children are also welcome in the pub. Food is available 12.00-14.00 and 18.00-21.00 seven days. The menu ranges from steak and kidney pie to grills, salads and steaks, There is a children's menu. The pub has a small car park which is usually locked outside opening hours: walkers may only leave their cars by prior arrangement (01948-3274).

Background

The origins of Marbury go back to Anglo-Saxon times when settlers built a stockaded village between two meres and called it mere-burg – the fort by the lake. Marbury today is a peaceful little village set in rolling countryside. The village's most attractive feature is the view of its ornate 15th century parish church perched on its hill overlooking the Big Mere. The church has some excellent gargoyles outside and inside there is an attractive fifteenth century pulpit, said to be the second oldest in Cheshire. The hills around Marbury are formed of unstable glacial deposits and the church has suffered subsidence and, as a result, the whole building is tilted slightly to the south, The tower is about 25" out of true and, inside, the pillars of the main arcade can also be seen to be leaning to the south. By the south-east corner of the churchyard is the whitened trunk of a long dead elm, said to be 1000 years old. Local tradition has it that if the elm should fall, then so will the church: the elm has been chained up, just to be on the safe side.

Marbury has another notable tree: a handsome oak on the village green which was planted to celebrate Wellington's victory over the French at the battle of Orthez in 1814. The village green used to be the scene of local festivities, the Marbury Wakes, which were held every October. The occasion was marked by the baking of a special

Marbury Church and Big Mere

Marbury Wakes pudding. Dancing bears are said to have been one of the main attractions at the wakes. Today, the village celebrates a Marbury Merrie Day in May. At the beginning of the century Marbury was a self-sufficient community with a post office, a communal bakehouse (in the Swan Inn), a malthouse, a wheelwright, smithy, a cobbler, a tailor, a school and five pubs. These, save one of the pubs and the post office, have all gone now but by way of compensation the village received piped drinking water in 1936 and mains electricity in 1951. In 1929 the village also acquired a men's club. It was donated to the village by a local landowner on condition that women should be allowed in one night a week. It now serves as the village hall.

Marbury's two meres are quite different in character. Little Mere is reed fringed and secluded behind a ring of trees: Big Mere is wide open and dotted with flocks of wildfowl. Like many of the meres in this area Big Mere is subject to 'blooms' of green algae which turn the water opaque in summer. Locally, this is known as 'the breaking of the meres'. Big Mere has abundant wildfowl. Great crested grebes, coots, moorhens, mallard, heron and Canada geese are regular inhabitants of the mere and several species of duck winter on the mere, which rarely freezes.

About half the length of this walk is along the Llangollen branch of the Shropshire Union canal. This was finished in 1805 as part of a plan, never completed, to link Shrewsbury to the Mersey. The canal was used by local farmers for feed deliveries as late as the 1920s and in its heyday it carried most of the area's Cheshire cheeses to market. Farmers preferred to transport their cheeses on the canal as they thought the water kept them cool and fresh.

The Walk

Most of this walk is along easy field and canal side paths but it also involves a fairly steep climb of about ¾ mile which can get very muddy in places.

Leave the village in the direction of Wrenbury, passing tree fringed Little Mere on the right. After a couple of hundred yards cross the stile on the left and walk alongside the field edge and over a stile into a large field. Go left and follow the field edge gently uphill at first and when you crest the hill strike out a little to the right to the next stile (a little to the left of the prominent tree). To the south-east Viscount Combermere's monument is prominent on the horizon. Combermere, who died in 1865, served with distinction in the Napoleonic Wars and later in India and so has more right to his obelisk than most monument-building aristocrats, who deserve to be remembered only for exploiting their tenants. The monument was used as a look-out post by local Home Guard fire-watchers during the last war.

Expect the path in the next field to have been ploughed up and not restored. At the bottom of the field you will see three trees in a line: head for these and the stile is by a gate just beyond, Then cross another field to a lane by Church Bridge lock, cross the bridge and turn left onto the tow-path. The next three miles of the route are a simple stroll along the canal bank. For much of its length the tow-path is rich in wildflowers in summer and you may see large numbers of dragonflies and butterflies. A particularly attractive section is between Church Bridge and Steer Bridge where for ¼ mile the path is overhung by a line of drooping larches.

After passing under Quoisley Bridge (easily identified by the traffic noise from the A49 and a '25' number plate) you pass Quoisley Lock. Continue down the tow-path, attractively reed fringed for much its length, as far as the Willey Moor Lock Tavern, Cross to other side of the lock but don't go down into the pub car park: at the far end of the lock a footbridge crosses an overflow channel and leads to a stile into a field.

Keeping to the edge, cross the field to the A44. Turn right for a few yards and cross over and walk up the lane opposite running uphill from the wildfowl sanctuary. After about 450 yards the lane ends at a house with a garden pond and turns into a hedge-lined bridle track, After wet weather this track is very muddy and the higher you get the muddier it seems to get. There is only one point of possible confusion on this part of the route. About 500 yards from the lane end the track divides but the right of way is clearly

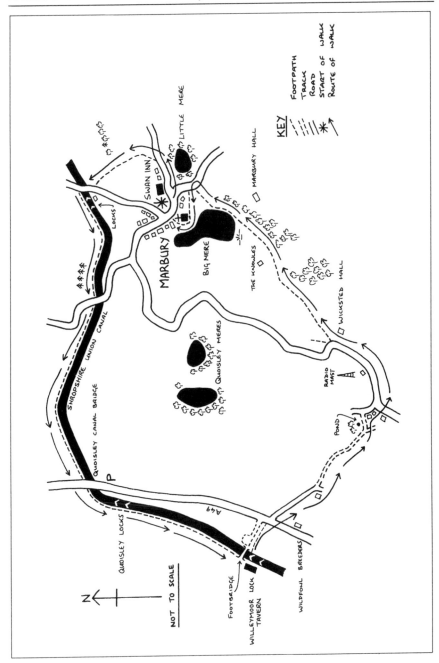

KEY

FOOTPATH
TRACK
ROAD
START OF WALK
ROUTE OF WALK

LITTLE MERE
MARBURY HALL
SWAN INN
MARBURY
BIG MERE
THE KNOWLES
WICKSTED HALL
RADIO MAST
QUOISLEY MERES
POND
LOCKS
SHROPSHIRE UNION CANAL
QUOISLEY CANAL BRIDGE
P
QUOISLEY LOCKS
A49
WILDFOWL BREEDERS
WILLEYMOOR LOCK TAVERN
FOOTBRIDGE
NOT TO SCALE
N

signposted as going to the left. You leave the worst of the mud behind at this point. Continue past a dark pond on your left and then turn right past 'The Spinney' to reach a metalled lane a few yards further on at 'The Paddocks'. All the climbing is now over.

Turn left down this lane and follow it as far as Wicksted Hall. The summit of the hill, a few hundred yards away to the left, was occupied by a signal station in the Roman period; one of a chain between the fortresses at Shrewsbury and Chester. No remains are visible but its modern successor, a steel radio mast, is, unfortunately, all too obvious. At Wicksted Hall, the road bends sharp left and right on the corner is a stile by a gate. Cross it and start enjoying the marvellous view over the meres, hills and pastures of south Cheshire which opens up ahead. The height here is about 465ft above sea level. Follow the side of the field and over a stile by an iron gate. Now head straight downhill in the direction of Marbury church and Big Mere. After another stile, the slope begins to ease and the path comes out into a shallow valley: continue along the valley bottom and cross a stile overlooked by 'The Knowles'. Keep to the edge of this field, which is wet in places, and over another stile to reach the edge of Big Mere.

The mereside path is wet in places but there are fine views over the lake to the church. At the next stile the path bears away from the mereside towards a stile by a gate. Cross this onto a metalled lane. Turn left here and walk down the lane towards Marbury. After about a hundred yards go through a small gate on the left and follow the edge of the field up to the parish church (a terrace with memorial benches in the south-west corner of the churchyard has a nice view over the lake and is an excellent place to eat your sandwiches if you're not planning on eating in the pub). After looking round this very attractive small church, leave the churchyard by the north gate and turn right on the road to return to the Swan Inn.

8. Around Hanmer Mere

Distance: Allow 2 hours for this 4 mile walk

Maps: Landranger 1:50,000 – 126 Pathfinder 1:25,000 – 828 (SJ 43/53)

Map reference of start/finish: SJ 455348

How to get there

From Chester: Leave Chester on the B5130 to its junction with the A534. Turn right and after a mile turn left back onto the B5130. At the traffic lights at Cross Lanes turn left on the A525 and after two miles turn left into Bangor-is-y-coed. In the centre of Bangor turn left again onto the B5069 signposted to Overton. At Overton, turn left onto the A539, heading for Whitchurch. The turn off for Hanmer is on the right, nearly two miles after passing the Dymock Arms at Penley. Drive past Hanmer church (where there is plenty of room for roadside parking) and follow the road round to the left past the post office to the Hanmer Arms about 200 yards further on.

From Wrexham: Leave Wrexham on the A525 and at Marchwiel turn right onto the A528, Ellesmere road. At Overton, where the A528 branches off to the right (signposted to Ellesmere) go straight on towards Whitchurch on the A539. The turn off for Hanmer is on the right, nearly two miles after passing the Dymock Arms at Penley. Drive past Hanmer church (where there is plenty of room for roadside parking) and follow the road round to the left past the post office to the Hanmer Arms about 200 yards further on.

Hanmer Arms, Hanmer

A large village inn, tastefully renovated in the early 1980s. Opening hours are 11.00-23.00 Monday-Saturday and 12.00-14.00 and 19.00-22.30 on Sunday. Beers include cask conditioned Tetley bitter and Burton Ale. There is also an extensive wine list. Food is available in the bar and also in the adjoining restaurant. The menu is extensive and ranges from steak and kidney pie to roasts (pork, turkey, lamb, duckling etc), seafood and various vegetarian dishes. The evening menu has many options not available at lunchtime. Traditional lunches are served on Sundays and breakfasts and morning coffee are also available. Price range is slightly above average. Meals are served 12.00-15.00 and 18.00-22.00 Monday-Saturday and 12.00-15.00 and 19.00-22.00 on Sundays. Children are welcome in the pub and in the beer garden. The pub was built in the early 19th century on the site of an earlier pub, the Blue Lion, which was burned down in 1820 along with seven other buildings in the village. Some of the outbuildings from the old pub survive and have been converted into hotel accommodation.

The Hanmer Arms

Background

Hanmer is an attractive village on the northern bank of the reed-fringed mere from which it gets its name: 'Hana's mere', presumably after an early Anglo-Saxon settler. Geographically this area of Clwyd is an extension of the Cheshire-Shropshire plain and the landscape, place-names and local architecture all show a strong English influence. The village is in the heart of the district known as the Maelor Saesneg – English Maelor – which was settled by the Anglo-Saxons in the seventh century and became part of the kingdom of Mercia. At the time the Domesday Book was compiled, in 1086, the area was considered to be part of Cheshire. The earliest known use of the name was in 1202 by which time the area had come under the control of the princes of Powys: 'maelor' is derived from 'mael lawr' meaning "the prince's territory". The English Maelor was constituted part of Flintshire by Edward I in the Statute of Wales in 1284.

The most interesting building in Hanmer is its church. The dedication of the church is to Chad, a seventh century saint who converted the Mercians to Christianity. Chad is said to have had a cell on the site of the church and is supposed to have baptised people in Llyn Bedydd, a small pool about a mile east of Hanmer. The waters of the lake are said to have acquired healing properties as a result. The association of the village with St Chad was so strong that Hanmer was originally known as Chad's Hull. The earliest records of a church at Hanmer come from the 12th century. It was in this church that the Welsh hero Owain Glyndŵr married Margaret Hanmer, the daughter of a local landowner. The church was burned

Hanmer Mere

down during the Wars of the Roses and the present church was built, rather slowly, between 1490 and 1570. This church was itself gutted by fire in 1889 and though externally it still looks pretty much as it did in Tudor times, the interior has been completely restored. Outside the church is a fourteenth century preaching cross. Scenes of the Crucifixion and of the Virgin and child are carved on the head. According to local tradition, the tomb set into the wall of the church opposite is that of the church's Tudor architect who is supposed to have fallen to his death from the bell tower.

Like so many villages, Hanmer is no longer the self-sufficient community it once was. At the end of the last century it boasted a butcher's, baker's, a malthouse (now a garage), a smithy and a saddler's. Now it doesn't even have a bus service. However, the village school is still open. Remarkably, it still occupies its original buildings which date back to 1676. The school cost £71 and 7 shillings to build and was funded by donations from local worthies (a shilling, denoted by 's', was five of today's pence). Fees were 1s 6d a quarter (12d = 1s) or 2s for pupils who were being taught to write in a 'book hand'. Pupils from poor families could be enrolled free at the discretion of the master. A guide book written by the local schoolchildren of today, available in the pub and the village shop, is a mine of information about the village's history.

Hanmer Mere, like most of the meres in neighbouring Cheshire and Shropshire, was formed at the end of the Ice Age when an isolated remnant of an ice sheet melted, forming a depression. The mere is now home to large numbers of wildfowl and several pairs of great crested grebes.

The Walk

This is an easy walk on quiet lanes and field paths through peaceful and well-wooded rolling countryside. There are few route finding problems as the paths are mostly waymarked. The walk starts with a little over a mile of road walking but, apart from a very short section on the A539, the roads are quiet and there is always a pavement or grass verge on which to keep out of the way of any traffic.

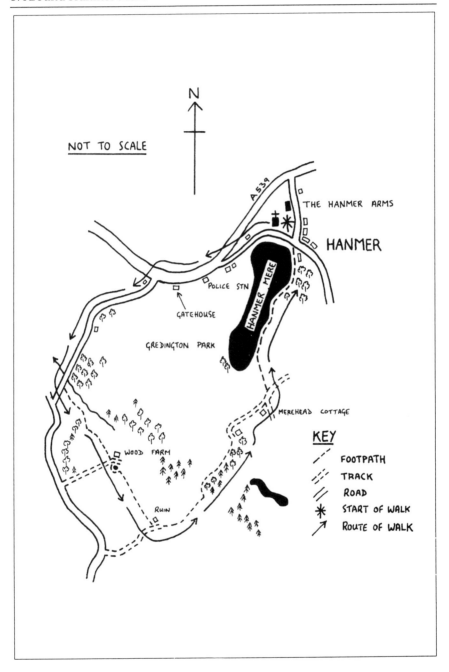

From the pub walk back down the road, past the post office, to the mereside and turn right. Follow the road past the churchyard, with its stately cypress trees, to its junction with the A539 nearly ½ mile further on. Continue straight on past the little police station and the gateway to Gredington Park and turn left onto the lane signposted for Breadon Heath and Welshampton. The countryside is rolling and the lane rolls with it: where the road begins to rise again just after the bottom of the third dip (about ½ mile from the start of the lane) look for a well-hidden stile in the hedge on the left.

This leads into a field; cross it to a wobbly stile just to the right of a bridge over a stream. From the stile climb the steep bracken covered bank ahead and at the top strike across the field in the direction of Wood Farm, passing between the two small clumps of trees in the middle of the field (the left-hand clump surrounds a marl pit). At the farm cross a stile by a metal gate and go straight across the gravelled farm road to another stile opposite. Cross this and walk around the sides of a pond and then, following the arrow on the corner fence post, head straight across the field towards a prominent nick in the hedge and cross the stile there. Walk across this field, between two isolated oak trees, to the hedge corner opposite and then, with the hedge to your left, on to another, rather rickety, stile. Some low ruined walls to the left here and a few damson trees (heavily laden with fruit in September) are all that are left of Werrion Farm.

Turn left on a muddy tractor track and a few yards further on you come to two gateways. Go through the right-hand gateway (look for the waymarks on the posts), bear left, and walk along the edge of the field, keeping a barbed wire fence to your left, through another gateway and, still with the fence on your left, walk down to the bottom of the hill. Cross a stile by a metal gate and go right along the field edge to another stile at the corner of a plantation. Cross this and walk uphill through fields with the plantation on your right. After about 300 yards, the path crosses a stile into the wood, turns left, and almost at once goes over another stile and back into fields. Continue on uphill with the wood to your right to a small wooden gate which leads onto a grassy track by a house.

Bear left along the drive and soon Hanmer Mere and the village church come into view. After about 400 yards and just after Merehead Cottage go through a small wooden gate on the left and, keeping near to the field edge walk downhill to the mereside. The route now passes through mereside fields (rather wet after heavy rain) and a young plantation of oak and ash to a stile by a row of estate houses overlooking the mere. Carry on along the reedy shore of the mere to a kissing gate back onto the road near the village post office.

9. The Dee around Erbistock

Distance: Allow 3¼ hours for this 6 mile walk (or 2½ hours for the shorter 4½ mile alternative).

Maps: Landranger 1:50,000 – 117; Pathfinder 1:25,000 – 806 (SJ 24/34)

Map reference of start/finish: SJ 354427

How to get there

From Chester: Leave Chester on the A583(T) and about five miles south of Wrexham turn off onto the A539 for Whitchurch. Turn right after 3 miles at the junction of the A539 with A528. At the Cross Foxes, about ½ mile further on, turn right onto the Erbistock road and park in the pub's rear car park. For walkers not intending to visit the pub, there is limited roadside parking a few yards further down the lane on the right.

From Wrexham: Leave Wrexham on the A525 heading for Whitchurch. At Marchwiel turn right onto the A528 Ellesmere road and follow it for just over three miles to the Cross Foxes at Overton Bridge. At the pub turn right on the Erbistock road and park in the pub's rear car park. For walkers not intending to visit the pub, there is limited roadside parking a few yards further down the lane on the right.

Public Transport: Overton Bridge is served by one bus a day from Wrexham, the 36 for Penley (Mon-Sat).

The Cross Foxes, Overton Bridge

Built in 1681, this old coaching inn is beautifully situated above the river Dee. The cross foxes of the pub's name are the arms of the Williams family, important local landowners. The pub is open 12.00-15.00 and 19.00-23.00 Monday-Saturday and 12.00-15.00 and 19.00-22.30 on Sunday. Beers include cask conditioned Marston's Pedigree and Burton Best and regular guest beers. Food is served 12.00-14.00 and 19.00-21.00 Sunday-Thursday and 12.00-14.00 and 19.00-21.30 Friday-Saturday. The menu includes Cumberland sausage, chicken breast, pork chops, steaks, salmon, local trout and daily specials. Sandwiches are also served. Prices are about average. The pub has a children's room and there is a special children's menu. There is a beer garden with a good view over the river. Customers may leave their cars in the car park at the rear of pub while they go for a walk but should ask permission of the landlord first.

Background

The walk starts at Overton Bridge. There has been a bridge here since the late 17th century and old engravings show that the original bridge was a picturesque three-arched structure. By the beginning of the 19th century this bridge was becoming dangerous and in 1810 the magistrates of Flintshire and Denbighshire met in the Cross Foxes to agree plans for a new bridge. One proposal they considered was for an iron bridge, submitted by the engineer William Hazledine who was later to build an iron bridge over the Dee at Aldford (see walk 19). However, they agreed to a design by Thomas Penson with

The Dee at Erbistock

a budget of £5000. Work was begun in 1814 but either Penson's design was at fault or his supervision of the bridge's construction was negligent because it fell down even before it was completed. No one was hurt but the damage was estimated at about £2000. Penson was sacked and the project was completed by another architect. Before the first stone bridge was built here, there had been a wooden bridge over the Dee about 1½ miles downstream near Eyton Hall Farm since the late Middle Ages. The decision to build the new bridge in stone was prompted by the high cost of maintaining the wooden bridge. Old accounts show that its timbers had to be replaced on average about once every eight years. This wooden bridge was strategically important enough to be garrisoned by Parliament during the civil war.

Erbistock is an ancient Anglo-Saxon settlement on one of the loveliest sections of the Dee. The name probably means either Eoppa's or Eorpwine's stockade. By 1066 Erbistock was back in Welsh hands, held by Rhys Sais, and has remained so ever since. The village is diffuse and if it can be said to have a centre it is around the small church on the banks of Dee, close to the site of the old ford across the river to Overton. The present church dates from 1861 but there have been several churches on the same site since the Middle Ages. A little further along the river bank is the 17th century Boat Inn (now a restaurant). Up to 1937 a ferry operated from the river bank below the pub. The fare to cross the river in 1897 was one penny, quite a lot of money to pay in those days. The ferry was attached to a system of ropes hung across the river and it was pulled back and to by a windlass sited below the pub. Some remains of this can still be seen. Coracles were still in use for salmon fishing at Erbistock in the early part of this century. Old photographs of the Boat Inn show coracles drawn up on the river bank. The fishermen worked in pairs, drawing the net between the two boats. Coracles were made by fastening hide or fabric (such as canvas or calico) over a wicker frame. A thick coating of pitch or tar made the boat waterproof. The technique probably dates from Neolithic times if not earlier. A small model of a similarly shaped boat, dating to the Bronze Age, has been found at Caergwrle, showing that such boats were used in the Dee valley for a period of at least 3000 years.

Coracles were just big enough to seat one and could easily be carried on a man's back. They were rather unstable and a large thrashing salmon could sometimes capsize a coracle and give the fisherman a ducking. This disadvantage was offset by the manoeuvrability which the coracle's rounded bowl-like shape gave it.

Erbistock is a quiet backwater today and it seems likely that it has always been so. The rector of the parish in 1791 described it as a community of 20 farms and 17 cottages with 'No family of note, No papists. No Dissenters. No Quakers. No constant and wilful absentees [from church] in this parish'.

Between Pont-Cysyllte and Overton Bridge the Dee flows in a narrow and deeply cut valley; in places riverside cliffs make it quite gorge-like. Geologically speaking, the Dee is something of a newcomer to Erbistock. Before the last Ice Age, the Dee turned south just east of Pont-Cysyllte and flowed in a great loop past Chirk and Ellesmere before turning north to rejoin its present course near Bangor-is-y-coed. However, during the Ice Age glaciers flowing down from the Berwyn mountains deposited huge quantities of boulder clay between Pont-Cysyllte and Chirk, completely obliterating the Dee's valley. When the glaciers melted about 10,000 years ago, the Dee started flowing again only to find its old course blocked. The water had to find some way out and it overflowed to the west, towards Erbistock, quickly cutting a new valley through the area's soft sandstone rocks.

The Walk

This is an easy walk along wooded riverbanks, through fields and on quiet country lanes. The soils hereabouts are heavy red clays and the paths do get very muddy after rain.

From the Cross Foxes, follow the lane in the direction of Erbistock. There are good views over the Dee and its wooded banks. About 700 yards further on, cross the stile on the left, opposite a road junction (look out for the public footpath sign). Go down a flight of steps and through trees to the river bank close to a weir and an old watermill. Now converted into a house, the present mill was built in 1602 but there has been a watermill on this site since at least the time of the Domesday Book. Turn right along the riverbank, through a small field and across a small footbridge into woods. Fallen trees across the path make awkward obstacles in places.

After about 400 yards the path comes out of the woods and leaves the river bank, crossing a field to a stile onto an unsurfaced farm track. Cross the stile just opposite by a gate and walk along the foot of a steep bank and then along a blackthorn hedge. Where the hedge turns sharp right head across the field, through a wide gap in a line of trees, and then, keeping to the left of another hedge, across to a stile by a metal gate (to the right of a new bungalow). This brings you out on a drive roughly surfaced with limestone chippings. Turn right and follow the drive to its junction with a metalled lane.

At the lane, turn left and follow it down to the river bank near Erbistock's attractive small Victorian church. Where the road bears right a track can be seen running down into the river – this is the site of an old ford. Follow the road past the church to the Boat Inn restaurant. Almost opposite the entrance, the path leaves the road down a flight of sandstone steps and then over a stile in a large pasture field. Keep to the tree lined river bank through this field. After about ½ mile you come to a stile which leads back into woodland. For the next 500 yards, the path sticks close to the river under steep banks and, in a few places, red sandstone cliffs. The path is wet and several sections are on raised wooden walkways to avoid boggy patches.

After crossing a rickety plank bridge over a little stream the path comes out of the woods and into pasture land. A wooden fence confines the path to the riverbank until you cross another footbridge and enter a small wood. At the end of this wood the path crosses a small stream (awkward when the river is high) and climbs a steep bank into a pasture. If you are doing the shorter alternative route, leave the riverbank here and cross the field towards two gates. Go through the red painted metal gate on the right and head for Lower Farm ahead with the hedge on your left. At the farm gate turn right to rejoin the main route. The main route, however, continues along the riverbank to a stile. In the next two fields the right of way lies

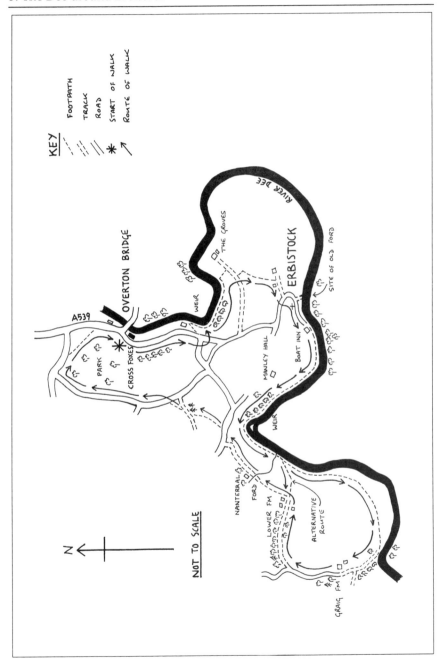

KEY

FOOTPATH
TRACK
ROAD
START OF WALK
ROUTE OF WALK

RIVER DEE

THE GROVES

OVERTON BRIDGE

WEIR

A539

ERBISTOCK

SITE OF OLD FORD

PARK

CROSS FOXES

MANLEY HALL

BOAT INN

WEIR

NANTERRAL

FORD

LOWER FM

ALTERNATIVE ROUTE

CRAIG FM

N

NOT TO SCALE

away from the riverbank along the foot of the steep bank on the right. At the far end of the second field there is a gate which opens onto a woodland track. Follow the track as it climbs through the wood to a gate where a track joins from the left. Continue straight on past Graig farm, where the track becomes a metalled lane. Stay on the lane (note the unusual iron fence-posts on the right) until a gravelled track branches off on the right and follow this down a narrow wooded valley to Lower Farm.

Go through the gate at the far end of the farmyard, turn left and continue along the edge of the field until you cross over a simple bridge over a marshy ditch. From the bridge head for the telegraph pole in the middle of the field and as you walk towards it a sunken way comes into view, leading down to a stile by a gate.

Over the stile you come onto an unsurfaced track which soon fords a stream by a cottage and becomes a metalled lane. Follow the lane uphill to a T-junction with a signpost for the Boat Inn and turn right down the lane for about 25 yards to a stile on the left marked by a public footpath sign. At first the way goes along a fence and a row of trees but when the fence curves away to the left continue straight across the field to a stile. After crossing this, head for the left-hand edge of the small pine plantation ahead where there is a stile onto a metalled farm track. Turn right and a few yards further on cross the stile on the left by a metal gate. Walk across the field to a gate in a hedge (look for the public footpath signpost) which leads onto a metalled lane. This gate looks like it hasn't been opened for years and it is easier to climb over it than to try opening it.

Turn left along the lane and follow it for about ¾ mile to its junction with the A539. The lane is quiet and there are wide grass verges most of the way. At the A539 turn right. After about 300 yards start looking out for a milestone on the left (it is nearly opposite a 'Give Way' sign). A few yards beyond this and well-hidden behind bushes is a stile which you cross into a broad parkland pasture. Head across the park to a wooden gate which is just visible in front of a red brick house. This gate brings you out onto the A539 again. Cross over to the footpath on the far side of the road and turn right for about 300 yards to return the Cross Foxes.

10. Wat's Dyke

Distance: Allow 3 hours for this 6 mile walk

Maps: Landranger 1:50,000 – 117; Pathfinder 1:25,000 – 806 (SJ 24/34)

Map reference of start/finish: SJ 337451

How to get there

From Chester: Take the A483 and follow it south of Wrexham. Turn off at the junction with the B5426 and head for Bangor-is-y-coed (i.e. turn left). The Fox and Hounds is nearly two miles along this road, just over 100 yards past the second turning on the right (signposted to Crabtree Green).

Public Transport: Walkers using public transport should start the walk at Erddig Park. Take the frequent Crosville services 1 or 1B to Wrexham and then change to the local 36 service which goes as far as Erddig Park in the summer only.

From Wrexham: The starting point of the walk is most easily reached by taking the Sontley Road (off Fairy St) to Gyfelia. Then turn left on the B5426 and follow it for ½ mile. The Fox and Hounds is just over 100 yards past the right turning signposted to Crabtree Green. Alternatively, start at Erddig Park.

Public Transport: Walkers using public transport should start the walk at Erddig Park which can be reached on the 36 service in summer only.

Fox and Hounds, Eyton

This is a small, quiet, plain unmodernised country pub. Opening hours are 12.00-15.30 and 18.00-23.00 Monday to Friday, 12.00-17.00 and 19.00-23.00 on Saturday and 12.00-15.00 and 19.00-22.30 on Sunday. Beers include John Smith's bitter and Ansell's mild. The pub serves food 12.00-14.00 and 18.00-21.30 Monday-Friday, 12.00-14.00 and 19.00-21.30 Saturday-Sunday. Typical meals include steak pie and chips, scampi and chips, chicken and chips, liver and onions, chicken tikka masala, gammon and steaks. Sandwiches are available. The prices are very reasonable. Children are welcome in the beer garden and in the pub if eating. Walkers using the pub may leave their cars in the pub car park: please ask first.

The Fox and Hounds, Eyton

Background

The main objective of this walk is a two mile section of the myste-rious Wat's Dyke, a lesser-known cousin of Offa's Dyke. The dyke runs 28 miles from the Dee estuary at Basingwerk, through Buckley, Hope and Wrexham, passing east of Ruabon, then through Oswestry before petering out near Maesbury. Nowhere is it as impressive as the best sections of Offa's Dyke and it is hard to get a good look at it because it is usually thickly overgrown with brambles and bushes. One of the best preserved sections is in woods at the southern end of Erddig Park: it can be seen by making a very short detour off the main route of this walk. The dyke probably gets its name from Wade, a giant hero from Anglo-Saxon mythology.

As Wat's Dyke runs to the east of Offa's Dyke it is usually thought to be an earlier Mercian frontier defence, perhaps built by Offa's predecessor Aethelbald (716-57). However, it might actually be later. It has been pointed out that Wat's Dyke follows a more natural line across country than does the Clwyd section of Offa's Dyke, which has many gaps in it and is incomplete. It may be that Offa's Dyke could not be completed in this area because Welsh opposition was too strong. Thus the Mercians were forced to pull back a few miles to establish a shorter and more defensible frontier. The fact that Wat's Dyke marked the English frontier in this area immediately before the Norman Conquest seems to support this hypothesis. It is also clear from a glance at the OS map that Wat's Dyke marked the linguistic frontier for a long period of time as English place-names are dominant to the east of the dyke and Welsh place-names to west.

Today, the dyke is rarely more than about 10 feet high but when built it was a much more formidable obstacle. Excavations have revealed that the ditch in front of the dyke, now shallow and boggy, was originally about 20 feet wide and 8 feet deep. The bank itself was built with the earth thrown out from the ditch up to height of about 6 feet. Then on the top of the bank there was probably a palisade of wooden stakes, giving the dyke a total height of 18-20 feet. The bank would quickly have become overgrown with brambles and thorn bushes making it even more difficult to cross. There is little evidence to show how the dyke worked. The line of the dyke includes the Iron Age forts at Old Oswestry and Bryn Alyn, north of Wrexham, but there is no evidence that they were garrisoned during the Anglo-Saxon period. This means that it is unlikely that the dyke was ever patrolled on a regular basis. The dyke was probably meant to be simply a passive obstacle to cross-border cattle raiding.

The walk just touches the southern part of Erddig Park which was landscaped in 1770. Erddig House, built between 1680 and 1715, is architecturally undistinguished: its main interest lies in the magpie-like character of the Yorke family who owned the house from 1735 to 1973. Over two hundred years they threw almost nothing away so the house gives a unique insight into the workings of an eighteenth century country house. The last survivor of the family gave the house and park to the National Trust in 1973.

The walk starts at the hamlet of Eyton which is part of the parish of Erbistock (see walk 9).

The Walk

This is an easy walk on quiet lanes, farm tracks and field paths. It can be very muddy in some places in wet weather.

The route starts at the Crabtree Green/Stryt-yr-hwch crossroads on the B5426, a couple of hundred yards west of the Fox and Hounds at Eyton. Walk up the lane towards Crabtree Green for about 300 yards, past a small chapel, and at the road junction turn right. A few yards down the lane, just past a rash of cottages, cross a stile on the left into a field. N.B. this is a recent re-routing of the right of way: a slightly different route is shown on current editions of the Landranger and Pathfinder maps. Follow the edge of the field across to another stile and turn right alongside the hedge, crossing a wooden fence which really needs a stile before going down a muddy bank to a footbridge over a shallow brook. Cross the next field by bearing a little to the left, up to a stile. Keep near the left-hand edge as you walk through the next field to a gate which opens onto a lane (strictly speaking the right of way joins the lane a few yards to the right of the gate but there is no way through the hedge at this point).

Turn left up the lane and after about 150 yards turn right onto the concrete track to Moreton Farm nearly ½ mile away. After going through the yard at Moreton Farm, the track becomes muddy and rutted. After 250 yards you will come to a cattle grid at the edge of Lower Moreton Farm. Turn left here, along the hedge and when the hedge turns sharp right head across the field to the gate in the far right-hand corner. Through the gate turn left and follow the hedge to a stile. At this point the route meets the course of Wat's Dyke – here only a low bank facing west. Don't cross the stile, turn right along the line of the dyke.

Route finding for the next two miles is easy. At first the dyke is not very well-defined but the way is clear as the path heads straight on through fields, keeping mostly to the right of the dyke but occasionally running on its low crest. When the cottage at Black Brook Bridge is reached, head round its right-hand side to reach the B5426. Go straight across the road to pick up the line of the dyke again which now shows a more pronounced drop towards the west. There are good views out to the heather moors of Ruabon Mountain.

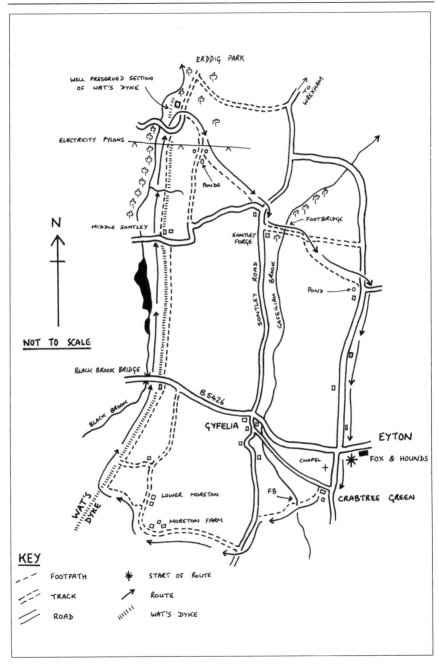

ERDDIG PARK

WELL PRESERVED SECTION
OF WAT'S DYKE

TO WREXHAM

ELECTRICITY PYLONS

PONDS

FOOTBRIDGE

N

MIDDLE SONTLEY

SONTLEY
FORGE

SONTLEY ROAD

GEGEILIAN BROOK

POND

NOT TO SCALE

BLACK BROOK BRIDGE

BLACK BROOK

B 5426

GYFELIA

EYTON

FOX & HOUNDS

CHAPEL

CRABTREE GREEN

WAT'S DYKE

LOWER MORETON

FB

MORETON FARM

KEY

- - -   FOOTPATH   ✳   START OF ROUTE

-‗‗-   TRACK   ↗   ROUTE

═══   ROAD   ⁙⁙⁙⁙   WAT'S DYKE

On reaching the lane at Middle Sontley farm, turn left and then cross the stile on the right just past the barn into a wet field. The route now keeps to the left of the dyke which is now a pronounced bank about 10 feet high. At one point there is a break in the dyke where a small stream passes through, giving a chance to see a cross-section of the dyke.

Just after passing under some electricity cables, go through a gate on the right and follow the iron fence on your left up to an inconspicuous and unusual stile. Now turn left along the lane for 100 yards to the cattle grid by the attractive little gatehouse cottage of Erddig Park. If you go into the park and walk into the wood at the back of cottage you will see one of the better preserved sections of Wat's Dyke. Otherwise, before crossing the cattle grid go over the stile on the right by a wooden gate back into fields and away from the course of the dyke. Follow the field edge as it curves round to a wooden gate. After going through the gate, you continue on the grassy track for about 100 yards until the track forks between three small ponds. Take the left-hand branch for a few yards before crossing a stile on the right near a gateway.

Strike a diagonal line across the field to a stile in the hedge by an oak tree. Head across the next field to a gate in the far right-hand corner, bringing you out onto a lane. Turn left and at the road junction turn right in the direction of Gyfelia and then, after about 150 yards, turn left onto the track signposted 'unsuitable for motors' at Sontley Forge. The track goes downhill between high banks to a footbridge over the Gefeiliau Brook. Continue on the track uphill for about 200 yards to a signposted stile on the right. Cross into the field and keep fairly near to the right-hand hedge as you walk across to another stile (watch out for the ditch on the other side). Cross the next field by heading left of the pylon to reach another stile which you cross into a small field. Follow the edge of the field round, past a gate to a rickety stile by a pond. This brings you to a lane: turn right and follow the lane, which carries little traffic, for nearly a mile back to the starting point.

11. Selattyn and Offa's Dyke

Distance: Allow 4 hours for this 6¾ mile walk (or 2½ hours for the shorter 4¾ mile alternative).

Maps: Landranger 1:50,000 – 126; Pathfinder 1:25,000 – 827 (SJ 23/33)

Map reference of start/finish: 267340

How to get there

From Chester: Though this is the most distant walk from Chester in this book, most of the journey is on fast roads and Selattyn can easily be reached in 35-45 minutes, depending on traffic. Leave Chester for Wrexham and then Oswestry on the A483 and A5. At the roundabout immediately after the A5 crosses the River Ceiriog (i.e. the junction between the A5 and the B5070 from Ellesmere) turn off to the right on the minor road signposted to Weston Rhyn and Quinta. Follow the road straight through Weston Rhyn (from where Selattyn is signposted) and about 1¼ miles after passing the Butcher's Arms the road makes a sharp turn to the left just before coming to a 'T' junction. Turn right here and few yards further on the right is the Cross Keys.

From Wrexham: Leave Wrexham for Oswestry on the A483 and A5. At the roundabout immediately after the A5 crosses the River Ceiriog (i.e. the junction between the A5 and the B5070 from Ellesmere) turn off to the right on the minor road signposted to Weston Rhyn and Quinta. Follow the road straight through Weston Rhyn (from where Selattyn is signposted) and about 1¼ miles after passing the Butcher's Arms the road makes a sharp turn to the left just before coming to a 'T' junction. Turn right here and few yards further on the right is the Cross Keys.

The Cross Keys, Selattyn

A delightful, unspoiled country pub: walkers will like especially the cosy low-beamed bar with its tiled floor and log fire. Built in the 17th century as a farmhouse, the building became a pub around 1840. It seems quickly to have become a lively nightspot as the landlord was fined £5 in 1843 for allowing drunkenness, and was fined many more times for the same offence in the years that followed. The pub is normally open 11.00-23.00 Monday-Saturday and 12.00-15.00 and 19.00-22.30 on Sunday but daytime hours may vary, especially in winter when it may be closed at lunchtime (ring the landlord to check: 01691-650247). Beers include cask conditioned Banks' bitter and mild. Economically priced bar snacks – soup, sandwiches, baps, toasties etc – are available throughout opening hours. There is a beer garden and children are allowed in the pub. Customers are welcome to leave their cars in the car park while they go for a walk.

The Cross Keys, Selattyn

Background

Selattyn is a small village nestled in a wooded valley at the junction between the Shropshire plain and the foothills of the Berwyn Mountains. Despite some unsympathetic modern housing developments, it remains a picturesque place, still very much centred on its 17th century pub and 14th century church. Though the place-name 'Selattyn' has a Welsh look about it, it is probably derived from

Anglo-Saxon 'Sulh', a narrow valley, and 'actun', a settlement by the oak trees (i.e. oak-ton), which certainly seems to fit the geographical position of the village. In the 13th century the name was spelt 'Sulatton', or similar variations, and the present spelling is probably the result of Welsh influence.

The village is only a mile from the Welsh border and it changed hands between Welsh and English lords several times before the present border was defined in the late 13th century. Selattyn was part of the Anglo-Saxon kingdom of Mercia c.774 when Offa built his dyke to the west of the village but by 870 it was part of the Kingdom of Powys. By the reign of Edward the Confessor (1042-1066) Selattyn was back in English hands but the Domesday Book, compiled in 1084, records that it had been restored to Welsh hands. However, by the early 13th century Selattyn was once again, and this time for good, back in English hands. However, Welsh remained the main language at Selattyn until the eighteenth century.

Selattyn church

In 1225 Selattyn passed to the Fitzwaryn family who held it until 1545 when it was sold to the crown in the shape of Henry VIII. Henry died two years later and in 1552 his successor Edward VI granted Selattyn to the Earl of Suffolk, the father of Lady Jane Grey who was queen for ten days in 1553. Suffolk survived his daughter, who was executed by queen Mary, by only a year. He opposed the queen's marriage to Phillip II of Spain and was executed for treason. Selattyn now changed hands several times until, in the seventeenth century, it passed to the Lloyd family who still have a connection with the village as patrons of the church.

Selattyn's church dates from the fourteenth century, though the fine sturdy tower was only built in 1703. The interior is rather plain, having been restored with a fairly heavy hand in 1891-2. The finest feature is its oak barrel roof which is mostly fifteenth century work. Over the years, Selattyn has had a few interesting rectors. One, Robert Staney was dismissed for 'heretical pravity'. Another Tudor rector, Richard Price, was convicted of harbouring a 'rebel' in 1575 and jailed at Southwark where he died in 1587. The most famous rector was Henry Sacheverell, a firebrand ultra-conservative fellow of Magdalen College, Oxford. In 1709 he preached against the recently passed Act of Toleration which freed non-conformists from criminal penalties and so finished up in court. Found guilty of seditious libel, he was banned from preaching for three years and 'banished' to Selattyn. He does not appear to have taken his duties very seriously and he left for London as soon as his ban expired.

It is quite likely that villagers from Selattyn were conscripted to build the local stretch of Offa's Dyke. No doubt they did the work willingly enough, living, as they did, with the constant threat of Welsh raids. The dyke is still an impressive obstacle but it would originally have stood over 20 feet high and had a wooden palisade along the top. Though the dyke would not have held up a full scale invasion for very long, it would have been a very effective barrier to smaller scale raiding: imagine trying to get a herd of rustled cows across it in a hurry, knowing that their irate owners will soon be in hot pursuit with spears and battle-axes. It may have been the intention to build the dyke all the way from Chepstow to Prestatyn but the northern section was never completed and it ends at Treuddyn (there is an isolated section further north near Whitford). It is possible that Welsh resistance was too strong to permit the completion of the dyke here and that one of Offa's successors pulled the frontier back to the line of Wat's Dyke (see walk 10). There are other gaps in the dyke further south in the Wye lowlands which, it is thought, were so densely forested that they did not need defending. There were no forts on the dyke so, unlike the Roman Hadrian's Wall, there was no garrison on permanent guard duty. The dyke may have been patrolled by horsemen though.

The few surviving records of the Mercians' border laws suggest that they and the Welsh often co-operated to help keep the peace in the frontier area. There may have been a joint board of Welsh and Mercians to settle disputes and there were recognised procedures for the recovery of rustled cattle. There also appears to be no truth in the old story that any man found on the 'wrong' side of the dyke would have his right hand cut off. There were in fact provisions for the safe-conduct of such people back to their own side of the dyke.

The Walk

This is an easy walk on paths and quiet lanes in rolling countryside typical of the Shropshire Marches. The route includes a well-preserved section of Offa's Dyke.

From the pub, walk towards the church and bear left alongside the churchyard with its magnificent yew tree and then go downhill past Yew Tree Cottage to a stone footbridge over a fast-flowing stream and a stile into a field. This little valley is the one from which the village probably gets its name. Walk uphill to the hedge and keeping it on your right continue up to a stile by a green gate and so onto a lane. Turn right and walk a few yards past two houses and a gate and look for the not very obvious beginning of a path on the right (it starts between a holly hedge and a manhole cover). This path runs downhill, becoming quite stony, through a narrow wooded valley, then past a nursery and cross the bridge over Morlas Brook to join a lane opposite a cottage. Turn left at the cottage and follow the track a few yards and just before reaching a gate take the grassy path which branches off sharply on the right. The path rises quite steeply uphill between mossy walls and overgrown hedges, turning sharp left and then right before levelling off before reaching a metalled track at Top Fron. Turn left and follow the track for about 100 yards, round a sharp right-angled bend, to a crossroads. Go straight across and follow the lane and when it bears left after about 200 yards (by an 'Unsuitable for HGVs' sign) cross the rickety stile by a gate on the right-hand side of the road. Walk past the quietly rusting petrol tanker – farmers have the cheek to complain about walkers' litter but no one leaves more unsightly rubbish lying around the countryside than them – to pick up the wide, slightly rutted, grassy bridleway. The way runs between very overgrown hedges of holly, blackthorn and hawthorn and is occasionally blocked by fallen trees which can easily be avoided by detouring into the fields on the left. There are excellent views over the Shropshire plain to the east. After a little over half a mile the track comes to an end at a stile near Fronheulog farm. Cross the stile and head over the small field to a gate between a rusty shed and an old railway truck. This brings you out onto a farm track. Turn right and a few hundred yards further on the track reaches a metalled lane. A superb view opens out over the Ceiriog valley to Chirk castle.

Turn left and follow the lane uphill for about 400 yards before turning right onto a wide grassy bridletrack. After a couple of hundred yards this becomes very overgrown but is still passable without difficulty. Offa's Dyke can be seen away on the right climbing the hillside out of the Ceiriog valley. After 500 yards the track reaches a gap in the dyke with a stile on either side. Turn left onto the Offa's Dyke LDP which the route now follows for the next 2¾ miles. There are plenty of signposts so there are no route-finding problems. Follow the dyke, which here marks the Welsh-English border, uphill to a metalled lane. The route continues straight across the lane and descends alongside the dyke to another lane. Selattyn can be seen across the valley in the middle distance. Turn left down the lane and after 150 yards turn right onto a grassy track which runs steeply downhill to Yew Tree farm where it becomes a metalled lane. Continue on the lane, crossing Morlas Brook near some old limekilns, and bearing left uphill to its junction with the Selattyn-Glyn Ceiriog road.

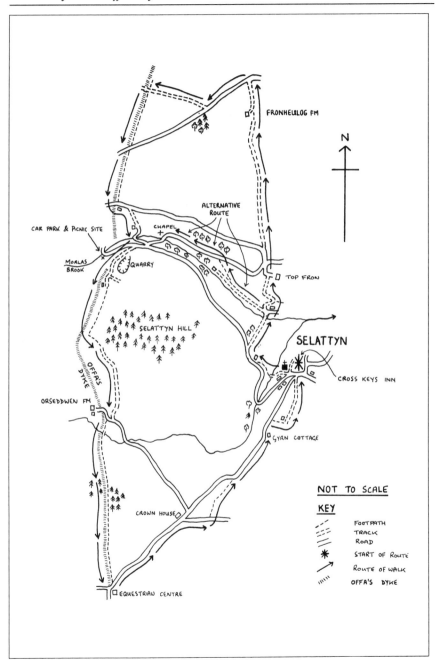

FRONHEULLOG FM

N

ALTERNATIVE
ROUTE

CAR PARK & PICNIC SITE

CHAPEL

MORLAS
BROOK

QUARRY

TOP FRON

SELATTYN HILL

SELATTYN

OFFA'S
DYKE

CROSS KEYS INN

ORSEDDWEN FM

GYRN COTTAGE

CROWN HOUSE

NOT TO SCALE

KEY

FOOTPATH
TRACK
ROAD
START OF ROUTE
ROUTE OF WALK
OFFA'S DYKE

EQUESTRIAN CENTRE

Turn right and walk along the road for a few yards and turn left onto a partly surfaced track (Offa's Dyke signpost). Follow the track past a disused quarry and where it turns sharp left carry straight on, over a stile by a gate, and past 'Woodside' where the track becomes a green lane running between ruinous walls. The prominent bank running parallel to the lane, 50 yards to the right, is the dyke, which here still marks the English-Welsh border. The lane rises steadily but easily to come out into a large open field near the summit of Selattyn Hill. Bear left across this field to reach a stile at the corner of a conifer plantation. Cross the stile and turn right on a grassy track which runs downhill, at first alongside a fence, and then through bracken. The track leads on to a farm track near Orseddwen Farm. Turn right towards the farm and then, at a cattle grid, turn left across a small field to reach a stile on the dyke itself.

The route now follows a well-preserved section of the dyke for the next three-quarters of a mile. To appreciate fully the scale of the earthwork it is necessary to climb to the top of the dyke and look down into the deep ditch on what was, from the Anglo-Saxon point of view, the enemy side of the dyke. The best section of dyke on the walk is reached after passing through a pine wood. In places between here and the lane at the Oswestry Equestrian Centre, the height between the bottom of the ditch and the top of the rampart must still be nearly 15 feet. A good view of the dyke sweeping down the hill can be got by a short detour to the right when the lane is reached.

To return to Selattyn, turn left at the Equestrian Centre, off the Offa's Dyke path, down a quiet lane and follow it for ½ mile before turning right at the road junction opposite Crown House (signposted for Pant Glas and Gobowen). Two hundred yards down the lane cross a stile on the left, near an ash tree, and walk uphill alongside the hedge. Just before reaching the crest of the hill, cross a stile onto the other side of the hedge, then continue for 50 yards to reach another stile. A good view out over the Shropshire plain opens up once the stile is crossed. Now walk down the steep bank to a stile and back onto the lane.

Turn right and continue down the lane and about 150 yards past

Gyrn Cottage go through a rickety gate on the right. The line of a track can be seen as a depression in the field: follow it uphill to a gate and walk right past an isolated cottage to join a muddy bridle-way (in wet weather it is probably better to stay on the lane). Turn left and follow it downhill, drying out and getting stonier as it descends between steep banks. Where the track rejoins the lane turn right for few yards down to the road junction and turn left to return to the pub.

The shorter alternative route follows the attractively wooded valley of the Morlas Brook up to join the main route where it crosses the Selattyn-Glyn Ceiriog road. Where the main route turns off to the right soon after passing the cottage by the bridge over Morlas Brook, continue straight ahead, through the gate, up the rutted unsurfaced lane, past a cottage and just before reaching a rather run-down looking farm bear off fairly steeply uphill to the right on a path which is indented into the hillside. After crossing a stile continue uphill on the path for about 100 yards but just before it goes through a gateway turn off up the steep slope to the right for a short distance to a stile which you cross to reach a quiet lane. Turn left and walk up the lane, through woods, for nearly ½ mile and shortly after passing a chapel you will come to the junction with the Selattyn-Glyn Ceiriog road where the main route is rejoined.

12. Castell Dinas Bran and The Eglwyseg

Distance: Allow 4 hours for this 6½ mile walk

Maps: Landranger 1:50,000 – 117; Pathfinder 1:25,000 – 806 SJ 24/34

Map reference of start/finish: SJ 242424

How to get there

From Chester: Follow the A483, past Wrexham, as far as the junction for Llangollen and Whitchurch. Turn off here and go right, onto the A539 for Llangollen. Go through Acrefair and about 1½ miles after passing the left turn to Froncysyllte the road begins to run alongside the Llangollen canal on the left. Start looking out now for the Sun Trevor which is about ½ mile further on, on the right above the road on top of a bank.

Public Transport: The Sun Trevor can be reached by Crosville Wales services 1, Chester to Llangollen (Mon-Sun) and 2, Chester to Oswestry (Sundays and Bank Holidays only), though the service is not very frequent.

From Wrexham: From Wrexham take the A483 as far as the junction for Llangollen and Whitchurch. Turn off here and go right, onto the A539 for Llangollen. Go through Acrefair and about 1½ miles after passing the left turn to Froncysyllte the road begins to run alongside the Llangollen canal on the left. Start looking out now for the Sun Trevor which is about ½ mile further on, on the right above the road on top of a bank.

Public Transport: The Sun Trevor can be reached Crosville Cymru service 1 (Mon-Sat) which runs from Wrexham to Llangollen at two-hourly intervals.

The Sun Trevor, Trevor

Situated on the A539, this attractive large pub was originally built as a farmhouse in the 16th century. The bar has an inglenook fireplace with an open fire burning in cold weather. The pub is open 11.00-15.00 and 18.00-23.00 Monday-Saturday (19.00-23.00 in winter) and 12.00-15.00 and 19.00-22.30 on Sunday. Beers include cask conditioned John Smith's bitter and Courage Directors. Food is available 12.00-14.30 and 19.00-22.00 seven days (from 18.30 Monday-Friday in summer). Morning coffee is available from 10.00 am. The menu offers a limited range of meals at reasonable prices. Meals include steak and kidney pie, sausage and chips, gammon steak, sirloin, chicken curry, vegetarian lasagnes and quiches, salads and a variety of sandwiches. Children are welcome in the pub and there is a special children's menu. There is a beer garden with good views across the Dee valley. Customers will be given permission to leave their cars in the pub car park while they go walking.

The Sun Trevor, Trevor

Background

This walk is dominated by the great limestone escarpment of the Eglwyseg Mountain. These rocks were laid down in the lower Carboniferous period, some 350 million years ago at a time when most of Britain was submerged under a warm tropical sea. The fossilised remains of shellfish and other marine creatures will occasionally be seen on the walk. The name of the Eglwyseg (meaning 'ecclesiastical') is probably the result of an association with Valle Crucis Abbey in the valley below. The plateau behind the escarpment is home to the ring ouzel, dotterel and other upland birds.

The other notable feature of the walk is the castle of Dinas Bran. The castle is in an advanced state of decay but the site is a superb viewpoint for the Dee valley which amply repays the fairly stiff climb needed to reach it. The castle was built early in the 13th century by Madoc ap Gruffydd, prince of Powys. The plan is basically rectangular, with a solid square keep at the east end overlooking the well-protected gatehouse. Compared to contemporary English-built castles it is rather old fashioned but its excellent defensive position must have made up for much of that. Nevertheless, no attempt was ever made to hold it and the castle was burned by its own lord in 1277 to prevent it falling intact into English hands. Around the crown of the hill can be seen the ditches and banks of an earlier, Iron Age, fortification. This was occupied through the Dark Ages and was destroyed by fire in the 10th century AD.

Many legends have been told about Dinas Bran. The first fortress is said to have been founded by Bran, the son of Queen Corwena (who, surprise, surprise, is supposed to have founded Corwen). Dinas Bran has some connections with the French medieval romances of the Quest for the Holy Grail. According to legend, the Grail (the chalice Christ drank from at the Last Supper) was brought to Britain by Joseph of Arimathea, the merchant who had paid for Christ's burial. According to the Grail romances the Grail was eventually kept at a castle called 'Corbin' or 'Corbenic'. Some Arthurian scholars have argued that, as 'corbin' is an old French word for crow or raven and 'bran' is Welsh also for crow or raven, Corbenic and Dinas Bran are the same castle: the old French romance writer has simply translated the Welsh name of the castle into his own language. Interestingly, Bran is also the name of a Celtic pagan god who owned a magical cauldron which may have become confused with the Holy Grail in the course of time. If Dinas Bran had at one time been a cult centre for the worship of Bran, then it might very easily have become associated with the legend of the Holy Grail in early Christian times when pagan customs and legends

Castell Dinas Bran from the Eglwyseg

were often Christianised by the church. However, the present castle is far too new to be the original Grail castle – if Dinas Bran is really where the Grail was believed to have been kept, the legend must originally have been associated with the earlier Iron Age fort.

Dinas Bran also appears as a 'castle of wonders' in a 13th century romance about the adventures of a Norman outlaw called Fulk FitzWarine. This story is set in the Welsh Marches and as the castle is called 'Chastiel Bran', the identification in this case is more certain. It is to hoped that there is no truth in this story, for, though many people went into the castle, only one was ever known to have come out alive.

The walk starts out along a stretch of the Llangollen branch of the Shropshire Union canal which was completed in 1805 by Thomas Telford. The canal was built as part of a grand scheme, never completed, to link Shrewsbury with the Mersey. This section was built mainly to act as an aqueduct for the rest of the Shropshire Union canal system. It draws water from the river Dee at the Horseshoe Falls near Llantysilio and carries it to Lower Frankton in

Shropshire where it joined a branch of the canal that originally linked Ellesmere and Welshpool. Most of the section between Lower Frankton and Welshpool is now drained. The Llangollen canal is very narrow and never carried much commercial traffic.

The Walk

This is a fairly strenuous walk in spectacular scenery with excellent views. About 1400 feet (430m) of ascent, some of it steep, are involved altogether.

Start from the pub by crossing the main road to the canal bridge opposite and turning right (i.e. towards Llangollen) onto the tow path. Walk along the tow path for about a mile, passing under the main road, and come off it at bridge 47. Then cross the bridge and walk up the roughly surfaced lane for ¼ mile to Llandyn Hall Farm and cross a stile on the left just before the road goes through a gateway. Cross the field to another stile by a gate and carry on uphill for 100 yards to a public footpath sign: turn left here and carry on uphill for another 100 yards. Then cross two stiles in quick succession and walk across the field, bearing a little to the left, to a gateway. Through the gateway, keep the hedge and fence on your left and walk past the farm to a stile onto a lane.

Bear left on the lane for a few yards and go through the green painted wooden gate on the right (public footpath sign). Keep the hedge to your right at first as the path passes through fields with views down to Llangollen. After about ¼ mile the path becomes enclosed between hedges as it passes first a farm and then a house. About 250 yards past the house as the path bends to the left, look out for a metal gate on the right. Go through this and walk uphill for a few yards and cross a stile. The ruins of Castell Dinas Bran loom above and are reached by a climb up a well-graded zigzag path that takes some, but certainly not most, of the hard work out of the climb.

Though the ruins of the castle are far gone in decay and give little clue to its original appearance, the situation is superb, with excellent views down into the Vale of Llangollen and across to the tiered cliffs of the Eglwyseg escarpment. The descent path leaves from the

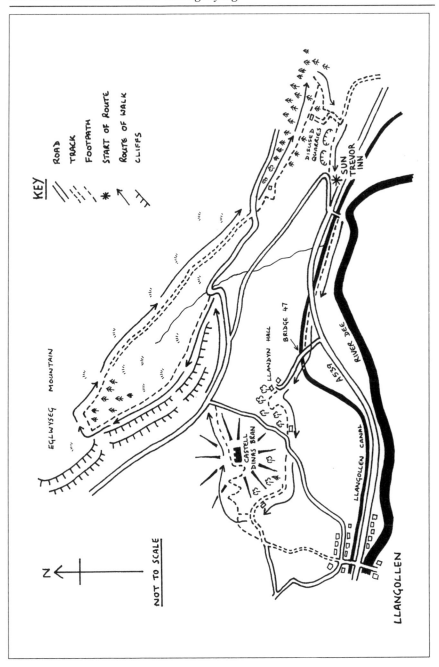

east end of the small summit plateau and zigzags quite steeply down to a stile onto a lane. The steep grass slopes of this section can be rather slippery in wet or freezing weather. Turn left up the lane for a short distance and at the road junction turn right.

The route now follows the road (which is also the route of the Offa's Dyke walk). After ¼ mile a road bears off to the right but keep straight on, past several old quarries, for another ¼ mile. At a sharp right-hand bend in a narrow valley take the wide path on the left (signposted Panorama). This is a 'permissive' footpath (i.e. a concession by the landowner) not a public right of way. The path leads uphill at a fairly easy gradient, crossing a patch of rocky ground, and after ½ mile reaches the edge of the Eglwyseg escarpment giving a sudden dramatic view across to Castell Dinas Bran and the Vale of Llangollen. The route now follows the edge of the escarpment, making easy progress uphill over grass. Just after passing the wind blasted larches and pines of the Eglwyseg plantation the path comes to a public footpath signpost at the top of a steep narrow valley. Turn right here, uphill, through bracken, for about 100 yards, alongside a line of larches, to a stile and turn right onto a broad grassy track. The track contours at first but after you cross a stile by a metal gate it begins to descend easily through gorse and bracken to reach a road after 1½ miles. The views down to the Dee are very good and the Wrekin is prominent in the view ahead.

For the next mile, the path is not always clear and a little care is needed in route-finding. Cross the road and walk past a green painted bench and then down a short steep slope to reach a clear path which bears left, gently downhill, through bracken. After 200 yards or so, the path becomes enclosed between a wall and a fence and enters a wood. At first, large fallen trees make this a bit of an obstacle course but keep near to the fence and the path becomes clearer after crossing a stile. After about ¼ mile the path passes above a cottage and about 200 yards further on it joins another path in a small stand of birches surrounded by conifers. Turn right and walk downhill, past a rusting iron shack, to a stile. A few yards further brings you out of the woods into a field. Cross to the right-angle corner of the fence opposite and then, keeping the fence to your left, walk 100 yards along the field edge to a stile. Cross this onto an unsurfaced road and follow it downhill for a short distance to a left-hand hairpin bend. Leave the road and walk straight on, past a disused quarry, and over a stile by a gate. A few yards further on there is a welcome public footpath waymark. The path now runs downhill to another stile by a muddy spring and then past a disused quarry (spectacularly overgrown with old man's beard) to reach a lane a few yards further on. Now follow the lane downhill for a few hundred yards to return to the pub.

13. Moel y Gamelin from Rhewl

Distance: Allow $3\frac{1}{2}$ hours for this $4\frac{1}{2}$ mile walk (or $4\frac{1}{4}$ hours for the longer 6 mile alternative route).

Maps: Landranger 1:50,000 – 116, 125; Pathfinder 1:25,000 – 805 (SJ 04/14)

Map reference of start/finish: SJ 182449

How to get there

From Chester: Leave Chester on the A483(T) and about 5 miles south of Wrexham turn off for Llangollen on the A539. Continue through Llangollen in the direction of the Horseshoe Pass (the A542) and about 300 yards after passing the entrance to the motor museum turn left onto the B5103, sign-posted to Corwen and Rhewl (N.B., signpost also for the Sun Inn). Where the B5103 to Corwen branches off left, go straight ahead and follow the narrow road for about two miles to the red brick chapel at Rhewl. There is ample room to park by the roadside here or continue for another $\frac{1}{4}$ mile to the Sun Inn.

From Wrexham: Leave Wrexham on the A483(T) and at Ruabon turn off for Llangollen on the A539. Continue through Llangollen in the direction of the Horseshoe Pass (the A542) and about 300 yards after passing the entrance to the motor museum turn left onto the B5103, signposted to Corwen and Rhewl (N.B., signpost also for the Sun Inn). Where the B5103 to Corwen branches off left, go straight ahead and follow the narrow road for about two miles to the red brick chapel at Rhewl. There is ample room to park by the roadside here or continue for another $\frac{1}{4}$ mile to the Sun Inn.

The Sun Inn, Rhewl

This is an unspoiled and atmospheric old drovers' inn in lovely surroundings: it is said to have 14th century origins. Opening hours are 12.00-15.00 and 18.00-23.00 Monday-Saturday (19.00-23.00 in winter) and 12.00-15.00 and 19.00-22.30 on Sundays. The pub serves cask conditioned Felinfoel Double Dragon, Bass and Worthington's Best. Food is available from 12.00-14.30 and 18.00-

22.00 Monday-Saturday (19.00-22.00 in winter) and 12.00-14.30 and 19.00-2.00 on Sundays. The menu ranges from sandwiches to main meals such as quiches, steak with mushrooms and onions, beef and beer pie, roast pork. There are also daily specials and a children's menu. Children are welcome in the pub (though not in the bar room itself) and in the beer garden and games room. If asked first, the landlord will usually give permission for customers to leave their cars in the car park while they go for a walk.

The Sun Inn, Rhewl

Background

At 1897 ft, Moel y Gamelin is the highest point on the range of hills, known collectively as Llantysilio Mountain, which stretches from the Horseshoe Pass to Carrog near Corwen. The meaning of the name is obscure but it has been suggested that it is connected with the Ffordd Gam Elen (the 'crooked road of Elen'), an ancient track which crossed the Berwyn mountains on the other side of the Dee. Geologically, this range forms a link between the Clwydian Hills to the north and the Berwyn Mountains to the south. The summit of Moel y Gamelin is a popular walk from the Horseshoe Pass but the southern slopes of the hill are relatively unwalked despite their great scenic beauty and excellent views over the Dee. No doubt this is due mostly to the lack of signposting, waymarks and stiles on the many public rights of way on this side of the mountain: something which needs remedying.

This section of the Dee valley was the heart of Owain Glyndŵr's territory and it was at his manor at Carrog, a few miles further up the Dee from Rhewl, that he was declared the last native Prince of Wales in 1400. Glyndŵr's name is even derived from the valley itself – Glyndyfrdwy: 'the valley of the water of the Dee' – and he would have known these hills well. Glyndŵr was of princely Welsh descent but he grew up as a loyal supporter of the English monarchy. Born in 1359, Glyndŵ r studied law at the Inns of Court in London before becoming squire to the earl of Arundel at Chirk castle. Here Glyndŵr learned the soldier's trade and went on to fight in Scotland for Richard II.

Glyndŵr's loyalty to the crown was probably shaken when Henry Bolingbroke overthrew Richard II in 1399 but it was a seemingly trivial property dispute that set him on the road to rebellion. In 1400 the neighbouring English lord Grey of Ruthin annexed a stretch of moorland which Glyndŵr himself also claimed. Glyndŵ r appealed to parliament but it found in favour of Grey. On 16th September that year Glyndŵ r's supporters proclaimed him Prince of Wales. At that time Wales was ruled from Ludlow castle with little regard to the interests of the native Welsh, who became more and more resentful of English rule. When Glyndŵr revenged himself on lord Grey by burning Ruthin, the Welsh people exploded into a general rebellion.

Castles and towns fell to the rebels and for four years a Welsh campaign of guerilla warfare almost succeeded in driving the English out of Wales altogether. Now at the peak of his success Glyndŵr dreamed of creating an enlarged principality of Wales, including Cheshire, Shropshire, Herefordshire, Worcestershire and Gloucestershire. However in 1405 Glyndŵr's attack on Worcester failed and thereafter the English began to get the upper hand. Glyndŵr's supporters began to desert him and by 1409 the rebellion was over. Glyndŵr evaded capture and spent the rest of his life in hiding among his native hills, finally disappearing from history around 1415.

Glyndyfrdwy was also the scene of earlier fighting between Welsh and English when Henry II invaded Wales by this route in 1165. Prince Owain Gwynedd barred the English advance at Corwen and forced Henry to retreat.

The Walk

Although quite short, this is a fairly strenuous walk with steep ascents and descents and nearly 1500 feet of climbing (1900 feet on the longer alternative route). These steep sided hills are well-drained and the going underfoot is generally good, though there are few places where the route is loose and stony. The walk is described in an anti-clockwise direction to minimise route finding problems but, arguably, the views are better if the walk is done clockwise. This walk is at its colourful best in late summer when the heather is in bloom.

From the red-brick chapel at Rhewl, head back in the direction of Llangollen for about 100 yards to a flight of brick steps on the left-hand side of the road (marked by a public footpath sign). Climb the steps to a kissing gate and cross a field and go through another kissing gate. Then turn right and follow the hedge to a small footbridge and a third kissing gate. Good views are already beginning to open up across the valley of the Dee. Head across the field, aiming a little left of the farm, to a fourth, and final, kissing gate and then up a grassy track, past an old chapel and some houses to reach a metalled lane.

Immediately opposite a grassy track leads uphill alongside a slate wall. Follow this for a few yards to a partly surfaced track and turn left, uphill. Where the track ends, about 400 yards further on, cross a stile onto the open hillside which is covered with bracken and gorse. The path now continues steadily uphill, along the edge of a pine wood. Though fairly steep, the going is not difficult. Past the end of the pinewood the views over the Dee valley really open out.

After ½ mile the gradient finally eases and a large spoil heap comes into view, and behind it the heather covered summit of Moel y Gamelin: it still looks quite a way off but two thirds of the climbing has now been done. According to the OS map, the right of way passes around the left-hand edge of the spoil heaps but as there is no path visible on the ground it is easier to continue on the clear path which passes through bracken and gorse to the right of the first spoil heap before bearing left into a 'pass' between two heaps. This narrows and the path crosses slate waste to come out into heather and gorse on the other side of the spoil heaps. On the right, the path passes a narrow rock cutting: this leads onto a ledge in an impressive, but still worked (therefore, potentially dangerous), slate quarry. The cleavage planes along which the slates are split can be seen very clearly in the quarry walls.

Once through the spoil heaps, start looking out for a faint path which branches off to the right. This soon becomes clearer. The path rises a little onto a broad ridge, crosses a boggy hollow and begins to climb steadily across the eastern flanks of Moel y Gamelin. The path is narrow but quite clear and the views over the Horseshoe Pass road below across to the Eglwyseg are excellent. After a little less than half a mile the path reaches the col between Moel y Faen and Moel y Gamelin. Turn left here onto the broad ridge path which follows the ridge of Llantysilio Mountain from the summit of the Horseshoe Pass to Bwlch y Groes. Though popular and well-used, this path is not a right of way but is subject to an access agreement negotiated by Clwyd Countryside with the landowners, the Llantysilio Estate. At first the path climbs quite steeply but as it nears the summit of Moel y Gamelin it begins to level out.

The summit of Moel y Gamelin is marked by a massive tumulus, probably of Iron Age date. The views are extensive in all directions but it is probably the mountains of Snowdonia away to the north-west that will hold the eye. Leave the summit by following the path in the direction of the prominent little Iron Age hillfort on Moel y Gaer (= 'hill of the fort'). The path descends steeply for 500 yards

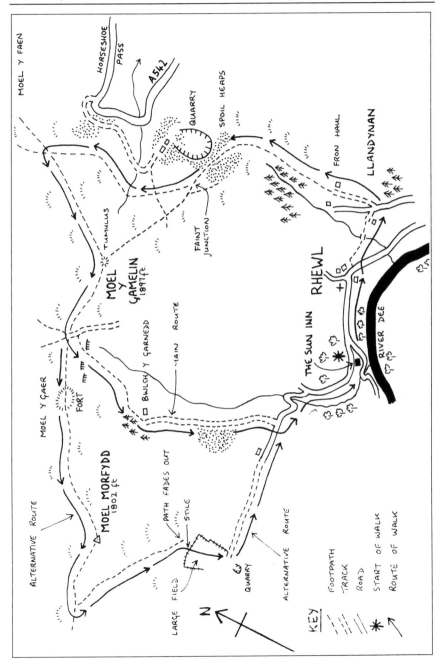

to the pass between Moel y Gamelin and Moel y Gaer. On the steepest section the path is very wide and has suffered serious erosion from the activities of mountain bikers and motorcyclists: restoration work is currently under way. On the way down look out for the line of the path to Bwlch-y-garnedd running through the bracken of the lower slopes south of Moel y Gaer.

At the pass, turn left along a cart track for a few yards and then bear off right to a stile by a wooden gate. Over the stile, the path descends steeply at first through a line of low broken crags and then more easily through bracken. In late summer this bracken is tall but it has not actually encroached onto the path itself and there is no difficulty in following it. The path leads down to a stile across an old wooden gate. Once over this the path runs between fences, with a pine wood to the right, to another gate which leads onto a rough lane at Bwlch-y-garnedd cottage.

The rest of the route is straightforward. Follow the lane, which is muddy in places, downhill through pastures for just over ½ mile to a roughly metalled lane. Turn left here. The lane winds pleasantly past meadows and woods, across a small mountain stream, and after ½ mile brings you out at the Sun Inn. Another ¼ mile of walking along the lane, with views across pastures to the fast-flowing Dee, brings you back to the chapel at Rhewl.

This walk can easily be extended to take in the hillfort of Moel y Gaer and the summit of Moel Morfydd. At the pass between Moel y Gamelin and Moel y Gaer head straight on up the broad but steep path to the hillfort. After a short descent the path begins to climb again for about 500 yards to the trig. point at the summit of Moel Morfydd. The path leaves the summit in a westerly direction, descending quite steeply at first before levelling off. When the gradient begins to ease start looking out for a clear path branching sharply off on the left, just past a footpath marker post. Follow this path as it descends diagonally across the lower slopes of Moel Morfydd. As the gradient eases the path gradually peters out and the next few hundred yards of the route are a bit tricky. The OS map is not much use as a guide for the next section as the right of way shown is completely overgrown with gorse and bracken. Instead, look out for a faint path which heads southwards through gorse and heather towards a field. The path goes down a very steep bank to a stile (this stile is a hundred yards or so further north-west than the point where the right of way crosses the field boundary according to the OS Pathfinder map). Cross the field to the far left-hand corner where you will come to a stile. Cross the stile and follow the path downhill alongside a fence. After a couple of hundred yards the path becomes a sunken and overgrown track. For the next hundred yards it is easier to walk in the field to the right but after that the track is clear. At Cymmo farm the track joins a metalled lane which is followed down to the pub.

14. The Upper Alyn Valley around Llanarmon

Distance: Allow 4½ hours for this 8 mile walk

Maps: Landranger 1:50,000 – 116; Pathfinder 1:25,000 – 788 (SJ 05/15)

Map reference of start/finish: SJ 191562

How to get there

From Chester: Head for Mold and then Ruthin on the A494 and one mile after driving through Llanferres turn left onto the unclassified road signposted to Llanarmon-yn-Iâl. This joins the B5430 (Wrexham road) after ½ mile. Follow this for just over a mile and, just after a left turn signposted to Eryrys, turn sharp right onto the B5431 to Llanarmon, about ¼ mile away. The Raven Inn is situated just opposite the church.

Public Transport: Assuming that you get the connections right, Llanarmon can be reached by public transport in less than two hours from Chester via Mold. Services 3, 4, B2, B3, B4 and B4X all reach Mold from Chester in 45-50 minutes. Services run at about 30 minute intervals Monday-Saturday and hourly on Sundays (when there is no connection to Llanarmon anyway). From Mold Crosville Wales service B5 leaves for Ruthin via Llanarmon at intervals of 1-2 hours (Mon-Sat).

From Wrexham: Leave Wrexham on the A525 for Ruthin and just past the Five Crosses pub at Coedpoeth go left onto the B5430 (signposted for Gwynfryn). Go straight on at the crossroads by the Moors Inn (signposted for Llanarmon-yn-Iâl), and straight on at the next crossroads at the Liver Inn at Rhydtalog. Turn left at the Rose and Crown at Graianrhyd about 1½ miles further on. The turn off to Llanarmon is an minor road on the left nearly a mile beyond Graianrhyd. It is a few yards past a 'bends for 500 yards' road sign and is signposted to Parc Farm caravan site. At the next road junction, about ½ mile further on, turn left and drive up the hill into Llanarmon which is now only about 200 yards away. The Raven Inn is situated just opposite the church.

Public Transport: Llanarmon can be reached by public transport from Wrexham only via Mold. Take the frequent Crosville Cymru services 26 or 26B to Mold and change to the 1-2 hourly B5 service for Ruthin which goes through Llanarmon (Mon-Sat). If the journey is planned correctly, Llanarmon can be reached in 1½ hours.

The Raven Inn, Llanarmon-yn-Iâl

This 18th century village inn is attractive outside and low beamed and cosy inside. The pub is open 12.00-23.00 Monday, Friday and Saturday, 12.00-15.00 and 17.30-23.00 Tuesday-Thursday and 12.00-15.00 and 19.00-22.30 on Sunday. Beers include cask conditioned Burtonwood bitter and Bass. The pub has a varied menu of bar meals and snacks at prices to suit most pockets. Snacks include sandwiches, bacon baps, many variations on the burger, ploughman's lunches and toasties, while main courses include fried rice, Chicken Madras, spaghetti Bolognaise, local trout and mushroom stroganoff. There is a children's menu and a separate restaurant menu is available in the evenings. Food is available 12.00-14.00 and 18.30-21.30 Monday-Saturday and 12.00-14.00 and 19.00-21.30 on Sunday. The pub has a family room and a patio beer garden. Customers will be given permission to leave their cars in the car park while they go for a walk.

The Raven Inn, Llanarmon-yn-Iâl

Background

Llanarmon-yn-Iâl is a pleasant small village in the attractive upper reaches of the Alyn valley. Today it is of no great importance but in the Middle Ages it was the capital of the lordship of Yale (=Iâl), one of the key areas in the English struggle to keep control of North Wales. Yale was originally part of the kingdom of Powys but the area was captured by the Normans in the 1070s and in 1086 it was held by Hugh of Avranches, earl of Chester. It was probably then that the impressive motte and bailey castle of Tomen y Faedre was built on a rock above the river Alyn at the edge of Llanarmon. The castle may not have been occupied for very long because Henry I granted the lands back to the princes of Powys after they submitted to him in 1114. Two hundred years later Llanarmon was back in English hands and the site of the motte and bailey castle was now occupied by the administrative buildings of the lordship. According to a survey of 1315 these included a great hall, courtroom, stable, store-house, cattle shed and water mill. The buildings were maintained at the expense of both the serfs and the free tenants of the lordship.

Llanarmon means the church of Armon. Armon is a local corruption of the name of St Germanus (or Garmon) of Man. Germanus was born in Brittany around 410 and, after spending many years preaching in Ireland and Wales, he became bishop of the Isle of Man in 466. He is thought to have died around 475. Many churches in north and eastern Wales are dedicated to St Germanus – perhaps reflecting his main areas of preaching activity. Until the Reformation, pilgrims came to Llanarmon to make offerings to a statue of Germanus which was dressed in sacerdotal vestments. The centre of Llanarmon is still St Garmon's church. The present building was restored in 1736 but most of the fabric, including parts of the roof, is medieval. There was an earlier church here before 1086. Inside is a fine effigy of a knight in chain mail armour, believed to be Gruffydd ap Llwyelyn ab Ynyr who died c. 1320. The effigy is said to have been brought from Valle Crucis abbey after it was dissolved in 1538.

Human occupation around Llanarmon goes right back to the Ice Age. Several caves in the limestone east of the village have yielded reindeer bones and the flint tools of Palaeolithic man while not far from Tomen y Faedre there is a Bronze Age burial mound.

Iâl was adopted as a surname by a local family, a descendant of which, Elihu Yale, founded Yale university in the USA in 1701.

The scenery on this walk is divided into two contrasting halves. Llanarmon lies right on the junction between the north Wales limestone belt and the shales and flagstones of the Clwydian range. The first half of the walk is on the rough pastures and acidic heather moors of the Clwyds while the second half is over herb-rich pastures and scrubby woodland typical of limestone country.

The start of the climb to Garreg Llwyd

The Walk

At eight miles, this is the longest walk in the book but, apart from a fairly stiff climb early on, it is mostly easy going. A few short sections near the river Alyn can be extremely muddy in wet weather.

Start by walking up the lane which leaves the village's main road just opposite the churchyard gates and to the left of the pub. After

¼ mile you come to a T-junction at a chapel. Cross the stile on the opposite side of the junction and walk uphill to a stile onto a gravel surfaced farm track. Turn right and follow the track up to the green farm gates. Go right here for a few yards to another gate and follow the grassy track up the right-hand side of the farm to a stile on the right at the top of a grassy bank. Climb quite steeply through two fields onto an open grassy hillside. There is no path but just keep plodding upwards, keeping to the left of the fence, until the slope eases just below Garreg Llwyd pass. The path crosses a stile onto the right-hand side of the fence and over another stile onto heather moorland.

A few yards further on you come to a gravelled track and a magnificent view over Ruthin and the Vale of Clwyd opens out. Cross the track and bear right down the path opposite for a few yards before turning left at the marker post onto the Offa's Dyke path. At first the path runs through heather, traversing across the head of a deep cwm. Ravens and birds of prey can often be seen hanging on the updraughts of air from the valley below. The path soon joins a rough track which is followed downhill for about 500 yards and at a gate, just above some sheepfolds, turn left (Offa's Dyke path signpost) onto a contour path. After about half a mile this comes out onto an unsurfaced road in the pass between Moel Llanfair and Moel y Plâs where the route leaves the Offa's Dyke path.

Immediately opposite are two stiles: cross over the one on the left and walk uphill alongside the fence a short distance, past two wind-blasted larches to a wooden stake. Turn left here and cross the field in the direction of another wooden stake before entering a small pinewood. There is no path but keep to the right of a low hump (the remains of an old field boundary) which runs through the wood. Shortly after crossing a stile in the middle of the wood begin to climb uphill slightly to reach another stile which takes you out of the wood and onto the open hillside (N.B. this right of way is not shown on current editions of O.S. maps and it replaces the right of way which is shown going through the wood from Tyn y Mynydd). Continue uphill for a few yards until a narrow but clear contour path comes into sight and follow it across the steep hillside and round a spur until a radio mast comes into view. Now head towards the mast on

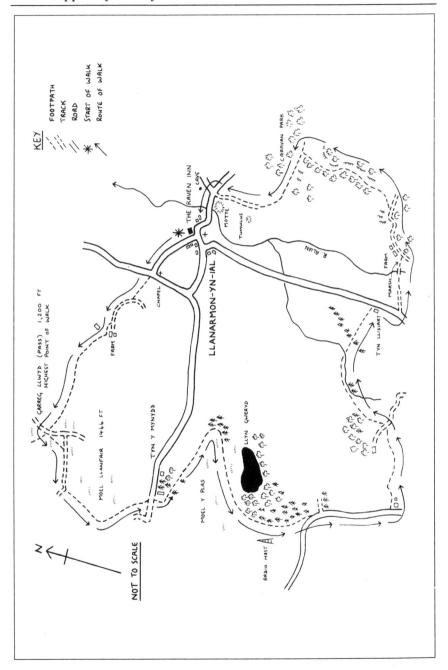

KEY

///// FOOTPATH
///// TRACK
——— ROAD
✳ START OF WALK
↗ ROUTE OF WALK

N ←+

NOT TO SCALE

CARREG LLWYD (PASS) 1,200 FT
HIGHEST POINT OF WALK

MOEL LLANFAIR 1466 FT

TYN Y MYNYDD

FARM

CHAPEL

LLANARMON-YN-IAL

THE RAVEN INN

CAVE

MOTTE

TUMULUS

R ALUN

CARAVAN PARK

FARM

MARSH

TYN LLIDIART

MOEL Y PLAS

LLYN GWERYD

RADIO MAST

an intermittent path which continues to contour across the hillside. Below, there are good views over Llyn Gweryd. As you come parallel to the end of the lake, the route descends a little to a stile at the corner of a plantation. Keep to the edge of the plantation and rejoin the Offa's Dyke path on the broad ridge. Keep along the edge of the rather windblown plantation, past the radio mast, and downhill to join a metalled lane.

Carry straight on along the lane, over a hill, to a stile in a hedge on the left with an Offa's Dyke path waymarker. The path, now clearly waymarked, runs downhill through fields for ½ mile to a tarmac drive. Cross the stile opposite (the Offa's Dyke path goes right) and cross the field to a gateway in the hedge opposite. Go straight across the next field to a stile by a multi-trunked sycamore tree. Cross the next field in the direction of a small conifer plantation to a stile on the muddy banks of a stream. Follow the right-hand edge of the next field to a stile on the right, cross the stream and walk uphill to a stile into a narrow pinewood. There is no clear path through the wood but bear a little to the right as you walk through it towards the light on the other side and you will come to a stile which leads back into fields. Cross this field to a stile in the right-hand corner opposite and follow the edge of the next field to a stile onto a road (marked by a public footpath sign).

Turn right and walk down the lane for about 200 yards and turn left onto the signposted public bridleway. At first the grassy track goes between hedges and after 200 yards goes through an open field to a footbridge over the Alyn. Cross the bridge and flounder as best you can through the quagmire on the other side to reach firm ground again about 50 yards away on a farm track. Go straight across the track and round the back of Pant-y-ffordd farm on a muddy path. On the other side of the farm bear right on the farm track which climbs uphill between drystone walls, through a gate onto a rough open hillside. Keep to the wall on the right until you come a small gate. Don't go through the gate, instead turn left and follow the wall a short distance over a low ridge to a stile.

Cross the stile and then keep to the left-hand side of the field and for the next half mile follow a long, very narrow field along a slightly sunken shelf between two low limestone escarpmemts covered with hazel woods. Towards its end the field descends and opens out. Head down to a stile in the left-hand corner and walk through a gap in a limestone outcrop and into a rough field by the side of a large caravan site. Keep the drystone wall to your right as you walk through a succession of enclosures of rough pasture, scrubby woodland and limestone outcrops. Once the path has passed the last of the caravans it joins up with the end of a neglected bridleway which runs between ill-kempt hedges and ruined walls. Llanarmon-yn-Iâl soon comes into sight over the valley before the track runs, muddily, between high banks down to a road below the impressive mound of Tomen y Faedre, a Norman motte built on a rock outcrop with rock-cut ditches. On the other side of the road is a large cave in a cliff above the Alyn. A flint arrowhead found in the cave in 1905 indicates that it was once home to prehistoric man. Turn left and follow the road across the Alyn and up the hill back into Llanarmon-yn-Iâl.

15. Limestone country around Maeshafn

Distance: Allow 3 hours for this 5½ mile walk

Maps: Landranger 1:50,000 – 116, 117 Pathfinder 1:25,000 – 772 (SJ 06/16, 773 (SJ 26/36), 788 (SJ 05/15), 789 (SJ 25/35).

Map reference of start/finish: SJ 202609.

How to get there

From Chester: Head for Mold first but avoid the town centre on the new by-pass, following the signs for Ruthin and the A494. The turn off to Maeshafn is on the A494, about 1 mile beyond the last roundabout on the Mold by-pass on the left, about 300 yards past the Rainbow pub. Follow the road, past a quarry, for about a mile and just past the 'Maeshafn' sign turn right into Maeshafn village. The Miners' Arms is just off the road down a track on the left about 50 yards from the junction.

Public Transport: Walkers using public transport should start the walk at Llanferres which can be reached by Crosville Wales' B5 from Mold to Ruthin service: buses leave at 1-2 hour intervals (Mon-Sat). For details of buses from Chester to Mold see walk 14.

From Wrexham: Leave Wrexham on the A541 and then the B5444 for Mold. On reaching the Mold by-pass follow the signs for Ruthin and A494. The turn off to Maeshafn is on the A494, about 1 mile beyond the last roundabout on the Mold by-pass on the left, about 300 yards past the Rainbow pub. Follow the road, past a quarry, for about a mile and just past the 'Maeshafn' sign turn right into Maeshafn village. The Miners' Arms is just off the road down a track on the left about 50 yards from the junction. Though it looks longer on the map, this route is in fact slightly shorter and much faster than leaving the B5444 before the Mold by-pass and going through the lanes via Nercwys.

Public Transport: Walkers using public transport should start the walk from Llanferres which can be reached using Crosville Cymru's B5 Mold to Ruthin service: buses leave Mold at 1-2 hour intervals (Mon-Sat). Mold can easily be reached from Wrexham on the frequent 1 and 1B services. If you get the connections right the whole journey should take less than 1½ hours.

The Miners' Arms, Maeshafn

This is a 17th century lead miners' pub, solid looking on the outside and cosy inside with a log fire in the bar in winter. Traditionally, the local miners were paid in the pub, an arrangement which no doubt pleased the landlords of the day. The pub is open 11.00-14.00 and 16.30-23.00 Monday-Friday, 11.00-15.00 and 16.30-23.00 on Saturday and 12.00-15.00 and 19.00-22.30 on Sunday. Beers include cask conditioned Theakston's Best Bitter, XB and Old Peculier. Food is available 11.00-14.00 and 18.00-21.00 Monday-Saturday and 12.00-14.00 and 19.00-21.00 on Sunday. Sandwiches and plough-man's lunches are served together with a range of main meals such as mixed grills, gammon and chips, plaice and chips, chilli con carne, vegetarian lasagne and broccoli and cheese bake. The price range is average. Children are welcome in the small beer garden and in the pub. Customers will be given permission to leave their cars in the car park while they go for a walk.

The Miners' Arms, Maeshafn

The Druid Inn, Llanferres

Built in the 17th century, this pub overlooks the Alyn valley and has good views from its dining rooms and terrace. Opening hours are 12.00-15.00 and 17.00-23.00 Monday-Friday, 12.00-23.00 on Saturday and 12.00-15.00 and 19.00-22.30 on Sunday. Beers include cask conditioned Burtonwood's bitter (N.B. the pub has two bars but real ale is only available in the top bar). The pub has a varied menu which ranges from sandwiches, baked potatoes and ploughman's lunches to main meals like steak au poivre, beef in red wine, chicken piri piri, gammon and Portuguese nut roast at average prices. Parties can be catered for. Children are allowed in the pub. Customers are welcome to leave their cars in the car park while they go for a walk but should ask permission first.

Background

Maeshafn (from Maes-y-Safn, 'the meadow of the ravine') is a pleasant 18th-century miners' village set in thickly wooded lime-stone country. The history of mining in this area goes back to Roman times or before. When the medieval churchman and travel writer Gerald of Wales passed through Clwyd in 1188 he noted that the area had established itself as a major supplier of lead and silver (an important by-product of lead ore). Maeshafn's lead mines, like many in this area, started working in a small way in the 17th century but large scale working started only in 1755. The veins were among the richest in the area but were soon worked out and the mines closed in 1799. Rising prices led to the re-opening of the mines in 1823 and the discovery of further rich veins led to a boom period between 1840 and 1865. Production averaged 80-120 tons a month in this period and, with the price of lead ore reaching £1250 for 100 tons in 1862, the mines were very profitable. However, the arrival of cheap imports led to a decline in the industry after 1875 and the mines had gone out of business by the end of the century. Many traces of the industry will be seen on this walk, including ruined mine sheds and many spoil heaps, but most of the workings are now very overgrown and hidden in thick woodland. In the twentieth century limestone quarrying has replaced mining as the major extractive industry of the area. The scale and pace of some of the quarrying operations is daunting: this part of Clwyd is fast becoming hollow and several footpaths around Maeshafn (still shown on current editions of the Ordnance Survey 1:50,000 and 1:25,000 maps) have been lost to quarrying.

The surroundings of Maeshafn are so lush that it comes as something of a surprise to discover that the village lies at an altitude of almost 1000 feet. The local limestone weathers to produce calcium rich-soils which support a rich variety of wild flowers. Botanists have discovered a number of rarities in the area including the woolly thistle, the green-flowered helleborine and the purple gromwell.

The Walk

This is a walk on woodland tracks and over rough pastures with one half-mile section of steep climbing. Some of the paths, especially close to the river Alyn, can be very wet after rain.

Leave the pub car park and turn left down the lane for about 100 yards and bear left again on the roughly surfaced track to Pentre Cerric. The track runs through dense birchwoods and, after about 300 yards, where the track forks take the left-hand branch which goes slightly uphill and becomes muddy. After another 200 yards or so start looking out on your right for a track which leads a few yards off route to a cave in the limestone (its position is marked by a green Forestry Commission 'keep out' notice). The cave has been excavated by archaeologists, who discovered human and animal bones, a Bronze Age arrowhead and a Roman brooch. The cave passage is quite high and, if you have brought a torch, can easily be followed (at your own risk, of course!) for several yards as it winds steeply downwards to a small chamber. A low crawl, partly dug by miners looking for new veins of lead ore, continues from the chamber for several hundred feet but further exploration is probably best left to the experts. Continue on the track for another 200 yards after the cave and turn right on a path that goes downhill through young beech woodland (doubling back a little on the way you have already come) to join a partly metalled track.

Turn left down the track and follow it to the gates of Pentre-cer-rig-bach where the path is diverted off to the left to come out on a gravelled track at a white gate. Turn right here and cross the field to a stile and cross it onto a grassy track which goes downhill between hedges among pastures. There are good views to Llanferres across the valley. After about ¼ mile the track comes to a bridge, crosses the river Alyn and then climbs up to the A494 just opposite the Druid Inn at Llanferres. The attractive church next to the pub was rebuilt in 1774 and further remodelled in 1843. Some traces of a medieval church survive.

Turn left and walk down the main road for ¼ mile – footpath or wide grass verge all the way – to a stile on the left marked by a public footpath sign. Cross a field to footbridge over the Alyn and then cross another field heading for the gateway in the far right-hand corner. Keep to the hedge through the next field to a metal stile by a spring and on past a long disused limestone quarry. The path, now a rutted track, begins to gain height slowly and just past Armon Cottages it joins a metalled lane. Turn right and follow the lane uphill for about 100 yards and cross the step stile on the left.

The path now goes steeply up a limestone escarpment, past old field boundaries and spoil heaps, through open birch wood. Just as the woodland begins to give way to bracken the slope begins to ease and soon after the path joins a rutted track. The view back over to the Clwydian Hills is excellent. The track continues uphill through limestone outcrops into a small cliff lined hollow before zigzagging up to the summit of the hill. The track now descends gently past old mine workings to reach a metalled road near a prominently sited underground reservoir.

Turn left along the road for a few yards before walking up the drive towards Fron Deg on the right (public footpath sign). Where the drive bends to the left, cross a stile into a small paddock and then over another one into a larger field. Keep to the right-hand edge of the field until a stile in the far left-hand corner comes into sight and then cross over the field to reach it. The route now goes downhill over rough pasture and bracken in a shallow valley. There is no clear path so aim at the white house (Coed Bach) on the edge of the woods

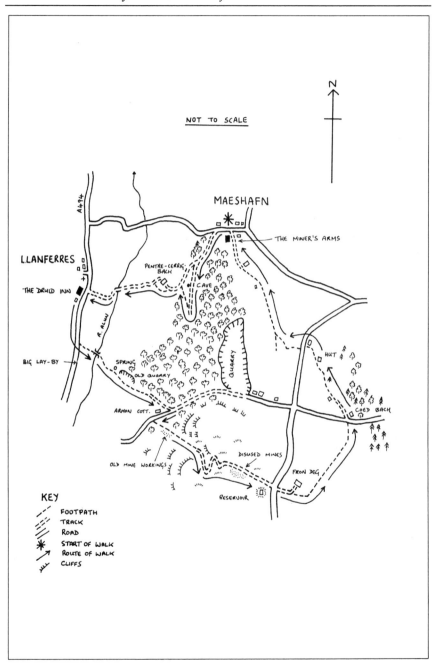

NOT TO SCALE

N

MAESHAFN

THE MINER'S ARMS

LLANFERRES

PENTRE-CERRIG BACH

THE DRUID INN

CAVE

HUT

A494

R. ALYN

QUARRY

BIG LAY-BY

SPRING

OLD QUARRY

COED BACH

ARMON COTT.

OLD MINE WORKINGS

DISUSED MINES

FRON DEG

RESERVOIR

KEY

FOOTPATH
TRACK
ROAD
START OF WALK
ROUTE OF WALK
CLIFFS

which can be seen immediately ahead. Cross the stile at the bottom of the hill and walk uphill to another stile and then, with a wall to your left, across rough pasture to a stile onto a lane just opposite Coed Bach.

Now go through the gate of Coed Bach, across the garden and over an awkward stile by a wooden gate into a wood of mixed Scots pine, birch and beech. Follow a grassy rutted track through the wood to another awkward stile into a field by a barn. Walk past the barn and along the edge of a field to another stile between a Scots pine and a gate. Cross the stile and at the bottom of the dip, a few yards further on, cross yet another awkward stile on the left and follow a track across some heathy pasture to a stile by a white gate near a Ramblers Association hut. Follow a path through a small patch of woodland and turn right in the field on the other side to reach another stile a few yards away. Cross the stile and turn left, walking along the fence down to the road to the left of the white cottage.

Cross the road to a public footpath sign a few yards away to the left. Go through the gate and follow the field edge and go through a red gate on the left, then along the right-hand edge of this field to some stone steps and a stile. Over the stile, climb the steep bank in front of you, bearing left, past a hawthorn tree and under some telephone wires. Head towards the quarry and look carefully among the bracken and hawthorns at the edge of the field for a well-hidden path which is cut into the hillside. This leads gently downhill to a stile by some sycamore trees. Cross the next field to a stile at the end of a low ruined wall. The path now runs through two fields in a pleasant little valley with woods on either side to a waymarked stile. Turn left over the stile and over another stile almost immediately. Then keep the fence to your left and walk through the field, past a small disused quarry on the right and over a stile and round the left-hand side of a white house onto a track surfaced with chippings. Follow this track down to the Miners' Arms again.

16. Loggerheads & the Leete path

Distance: Allow 3 hours for this 5$\frac{1}{2}$ mile walk

Maps: Landranger 1:50,000 – 116, 117; Pathfinder 1:25,000 – 772 (SJ 06/16), 773 (SJ 26/36)

Map reference of start/finish:

How to get there

From Chester: From Chester head for Mold but avoid the town centre on the new by-pass. Just over a mile after the last roundabout on the by-pass look for the turning signposted to Gwernaffield, Y Waun and Pantymwyn on the right-hand side of the road. The turn off to the Colmendy Arms, which is unsignposted, is about 100 yards past this road on the right, just past a small shop. The pub is about 200 yards up the lane on the left. As there is only limited space for on-road parking at Cadole, walkers not intending to use the pub may find it more convenient to start the walk from the Loggerheads Country Park.

Public Transport: Cadole can be reached by Crosville Wales' services B32 and B33 which leaves Mold for Pantymwyn at roughly hourly intervals (Mon-Sat). The more infrequent service B5, Mold to Ruthin, also goes through Cadole and Loggerheads (Mon-Sat). For services from Chester to Mold see walk 14.

From Wrexham: Head for Mold first on A541, then on the B5444 and at the Mold by-pass turn left onto the A494 for Ruthin. Just over a mile after the last roundabout on the by-pass look for the turning signposted to Gwernaffield, Y Waun and Pantymwyn on the right-hand side of the road. The turn off to the Colmendy Arms, which is unsignposted, is about 100 yards past this road on the right, just past a small shop. The pub is about 200 yards up the lane on the left. As there is only limited space for on-road parking at Cadole, walkers not intending to use the pub may find it more convenient to start the walk from the Loggerheads Country Park.

Public Transport: Cadole can be reached by public transport via Mold. The quickest way to Mold is the frequent Crosville Cymru service 26 which takes about 35 minutes. From Mold services B32 and B33 for Pantymwyn go through Cadole at roughly hourly intervals (Mon-Sat). The B5 Mold to Ruthin bus also goes through Cadole as well as Loggerheads but is less frequent (Mon-Sat).

The Colomendy Arms, Cadole

The Colomendy Arms is a small traditional country pub, only a couple of hundred yards off the busy A494 but a world away in atmosphere. It was built around 1813 to serve local lead miners. The pub is open 12.00-15.00 and 19.00-23.00 Monday-Friday, 12.00-23.0 on Saturday and 12.00-15.00 and 19.00-22.30 on Sunday. Beers include cask conditioned Burtonwood bitter and mild and Dent Brewery bitter and Ramsbottom. The pub serves sandwiches and bar snacks including sausage and chips, scampi and chips and the like at good value prices. Food is available 12.00-14.00 and 19.00-21.30 Sunday-Friday and all day on Saturday. Children are welcome in the beer garden and in the pub. The pub has quite a large car park and walkers using the pub may, with permission, leave their cars there while they go for a walk.

We Three Loggerheads, Loggerheads

This is a large, comfortable, food-orientated pub on the A494 opposite the Loggerheads country park. The pub's curious name comes from a painting by a local artist of two men at loggerheads – the third

We Three Loggerheads, Loggerheads

being the artist. The pub itself was built in 1750. The pub is open 12.00-15.00 and 17.30-23.00 Monday-Thursday, 12.00-23.00 Friday-Saturday and 12.00-15.00 and 19.00-22.30 on Sunday. Beers include cask conditioned Bass and regular guest beers. The pub serves meals from a set menu which ranges from sandwiches, ploughman's lunches and baked potatoes to steak pie, roast ham and vegetarian options. There is also an interesting menu of 'specials' which is changed daily and traditional Sunday lunches are served. Prices are average. Food is available 12.00-15.00 and 18.00-22.00 Monday-Saturday and 12.00-15.00 on Sunday. Children are welcome in the pub's dining rooms.

Also on the route is the Crown Inn at Pantymwyn. This is a plain village pub which does not serve food at lunchtimes except on Sundays. Greenalls beers.

Background

Between the 17th and 19th centuries the Alyn valley was an important lead mining area and considerable remains from this industry will be seen on this walk. The mineral rights in this area, which straddles the old border between the now-defunct counties of Flintshire and Denbighshire, were fiercely contested over many years and it is thought that these frequent disputes between intransigent parties are what has given Loggerheads its unusual name. In one 18th century dispute the son of the vicar of Llanferres was even accused of moving the county boundary markers. The county boundary dispute was settled only in 1763 and the agreement is commemorated by a memorial by the side of the A494 between Cadole and Loggerheads.

The river Alyn had a major influence on the development of the mines. By the 18th century many of the shafts of the Glan Alyn mine at Loggerheads were as much as 600 feet below the level of the river and so were very prone to flooding. The fast flowing river also provided the answer to the problems it was causing when it was harnessed to turn waterwheels to drive pumps to drain the mines.

Below Loggerheads, in summer the Alyn has a tendency to sink into swallow holes in its limestone bed and run underground for several miles. According to local legend King Benlli was punished for an act of wickedness by being made to feel as if he was burning all over. He tried to cool himself in the river but every time he did so the river disappeared and it has continued to do so every now and again ever since. The river's disappearances caused major problems for the lead mines downstream from Loggerheads as they were deprived of a reliable source of water power for their pumps and processing operations. To rectify this John Taylor, a Cornish mining engineer, cut a 3 mile long water channel, or 'leat', along the side of the valley from Loggerheads to Rhydymwyn in 1824. The leat no longer carries water but it survives as a footpath, known as the Leete Path, which provides easy walking and excellent views over the Alyn valley. Despite the exercise of technical ingenuity, working the lead mines remained a difficult and expensive business and they were eventually put out of business in 1872 by cheaper imports.

Mining operations quite often broke into natural caverns dissolved out of the limestone by the underground streams that caused the miners so many problems. The longest cave so far discovered in the area, the Ogof Hesp Alyn, is over a mile in length.

The Loggerheads area also has plenty of natural history interest as a result of the calcium rich limestone soils. The denser woodland areas have acres of dog's mercury and enchanter's nightshade as well as the more common woodland flowers. The more open areas are even richer in wild flowers: rock-rose, harebell, milkwort, eyebright, wild thyme, rose-of-Sharon and bloody crane's-bill can all be found. Dippers and pied and grey wagtails forage for insects by the river Alyn and, if you're very lucky, you might even see the electric blue flash of a kingfisher in flight.

The Walk

Most of this easy walk is on level paths through attractive woodland and limestone scenery. The woodlands are at their best in spring and autumn. Apart from a short section in a pine plantation there are no route finding difficulties. The Leete Path section can be muddy and wet after rain.

The walk starts from a stile at the far end of the Colomendy Arms'

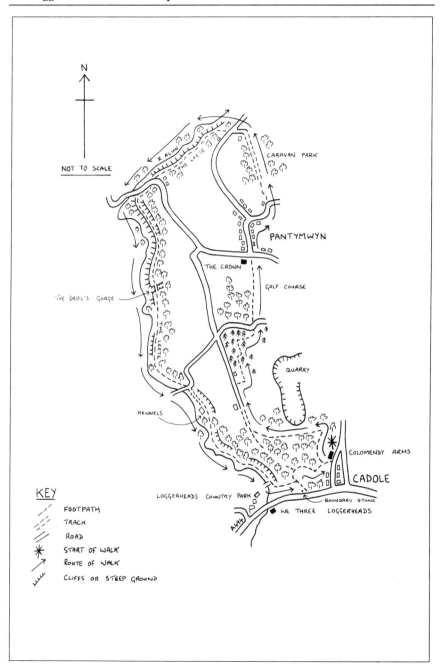

NOT TO SCALE

N

R ALYN
THE LEETE
CARAVAN PARK

PANTYMWYN

THE CROWN

GOLF COURSE

THE DEVIL'S GORGE

QUARRY

THE LEETE

KENNELS

COLOMENDY ARMS

CADOLE

LOGGERHEADS COUNTRY PARK

BOUNDARY STONE

WE THREE LOGGERHEADS

KEY
FOOTPATH
TRACK
ROAD
START OF WALK
ROUTE OF WALK
CLIFFS OR STEEP GROUND

car park. Over the stile, take the right-hand path which soon begins to rise gently uphill through woods to a stile. Turn left here, over another stile a few yards further on and then continue uphill on a clear path. As the path levels out on the summit of the hill a path branches off left into a clearing but continue straight ahead with a fence on your right. The path descends through dense, scrubby, woodland and it forks many times. Keep right at these forks until you come down to a wide level track by a 'Bridleway to Pantymwyn' signpost. Turn right, through a wicket gate and continue down the track until it becomes a metalled lane by a house after about 150 yards. Carry on down the lane, which has good views over to Moel Famau, for about 250 yards to a wooden step stile on the right by a green gate (public footpath sign).

The path now runs between fences in a dense plantation (which is not shown on the current edition of the Pathfinder map for the area), round a sharp left-hand corner to another step stile. Turn right over the stile and where the path forks by an old quarry notice turn left keeping roughly parallel to a line of telegraph poles, at first through pines and then along an overgrown forest ride. Near the end of the ride look out for a sharp right turn in the path – in summer when the bracken is high it is not easy to see – and follow it up a bank, through gorse and then under an arch of dense holly bushes to another old quarry notice. Turn sharp left here and walk quite steeply downhill through a dense pine plantation to a metal stile at a bend in a metalled lane.

Cross the lane to another stile opposite, walk past an old spoil heap and then along the edge of woods with a golf course on your right. Where the edge of the woods makes a sharp turn left, continue straight on across the golf course – watch out for flying golf balls – for a couple of hundred yards before following a hedge down to a bus shelter next to the Crown Inn. Now walk down Pen y Fron Road opposite and after about 250 yards turn left onto the road signposted to Llyn-y-pandy. After another 200 yards, just past Coed Mawr cottage, cross a stile on the left and cross a field with a fence on your left, across another stile and through a short section of woodland into a large caravan site. Though not unpleasant as caravan sites go, it would be greatly improved from the walker's point of view by a few signposts. However, just walk straight through the middle and out past a small playing field, turning left past Cefn Coed cottage and down to a lane opposite a post box.

Cross over and pick up a slightly overgrown path which runs downhill from the post box to join the leat at a bend. You will know when you are on the leat because the path runs in a groove along the hillside with a kind of parapet on the right. The route now follows a perfectly level course for the next 2½ miles. At this point the leat is about 100 feet above the level of the Alyn but over the next 2 miles the river bed gradually rises until the two are running side by side. For the first ¾ mile the leat runs through dense woodland but there are occasional views over the valley. Where the leat meets a lane, cross straight over to pick up the leat again, now signposted as the 'Leete Path'. The next mile is the best section of the walk as the Leete Path contours through woods across very steep slopes and even cliff faces in places. At one point the path bridges a huge chasm in the limestone rocks, called the Devil's Gorge but actually created by mining operations. There are excellent views over the river to the Clwydian Hills. A number of paths cross the leat but simply keep going straight on, on the level.

Where the Leete Path meets a lane, continue straight ahead down a drive signposted to Loggerheads (the leat is buried beneath the road here), past a boarding kennels and, a few hundred yards further on, through a kissing gate into the Loggerheads Country Park. Keep on the left-hand bank of the river past the remains of water wheel pits and along the base of high limestone cliffs to a two arched stone bridge. It was near here that water was taken out of the river into the leat. Carry on past the bridge along the base of the cliffs and then climb the steep steps up the hillside. At the top of the steps a stony path branching off on the left leads up to an excellent viewpoint at the top of the cliffs. The main route continues to the right along a well-made winding path to a junction with another wide path. A short distance away to the right the main road can be seen (a short detour here brings you to the boundary stone) but turn left, uphill, past marker post 15 and where the paths branch bear right and a few yards further on turn right onto the muddy footpath signposted to Cadole. The route crosses a stile in a low stone wall and through a clearing with spoil heaps to the stile into the car park of the Colomendy Arms.

17. Moel Famau from Cilcain

Distance: Allow 4 hours for this 7 mile walk

Maps: Landranger 1:50,000 – 116; Pathfinder 1:25,000 – 788 (SJ 05/15)

Map reference of start/finish: SJ 177653

How to get there

From Chester: First head for Mold on the A55 and then follow the signs for Ruthin on the A494. Two miles after the last roundabout on the Mold by-pass, just past the We Three Loggerheads pub, turn right into the narrow lane by the entrance to the Loggerheads Country Park. After about ½ mile come to a T-junction and turn right (signpost to Cilcain) and follow the winding and often narrow lane for 2 miles to Cilcain. The White Horse is at the crossroads in the middle of the village.

From Wrexham: First head for Mold on the A541 and B5444 and then Ruthin on the A494 on reaching the Mold by-pass. Two miles after the last round-about on the by-pass, just past the We Three Loggerheads pub, turn right into the narrow lane by the entrance to the Loggerheads Country Park. After about ½ mile come to a T-junction and turn right (signpost to Cilcain) and follow the winding and often narrow lane for 2 miles to Cilcain. The White Horse is at the crossroads in the middle of the village.

The White Horse Inn, Cilcain

A friendly village inn with an atmospheric public bar and comfortable lounge/dining room. The 16th century pub has changed hands many times in its long history; once, in the 1930s, as the result of a bet on the Irish Sweepstake. Opening hours are 12.00-15.00 (public bar 12.00-15.30) and 19.00-23.00 Monday-Saturday, 12.00-15.00 and 19.00-22.30 on Sunday. Beers include cask conditioned Marston's Pedigree and three guest beers. Food is available 12.00-14.00 and 19.30-21.30 Sunday-Thursday and 12.00-14.00 and 19.30-22.00 Friday-Saturday. The menu includes filled batches, ploughman's lunches and home cooked main courses such as omelettes, prawn madras, chicken and herb pie, Greenland prawn salad, steak and kidney pie and rainbow trout. The price range is average. No children under the age of 14 are allowed in the pub but are welcome on the patio/beer garden. Customers are welcome to leave their cars in the pub's car park while they go for a walk if they ask permission first.

The White Horse Inn, Cilcain

Background

The starting point of this walk is the attractive village of Cilcain. The name, meaning 'the nook of Gain', comes from a stream, Nant Gain (= 'pleasant stream'), flowing down past the village from the upper slopes of Moel Famau. The village's most notable building is its 14th century church, which has a finely decorated oak hammerbeam roof. The roof is said to have originally belonged to the refectory of the Cistercian abbey at Basingwerk near Holywell but was acquired by the church when the abbey was dissolved in 1535. There is no hard evidence to support this story but the huge angels on the roof beams do certainly look as if they were carved for a rather larger building than this church. The churchyard is roughly circular so, it is said, that there would be no dark corners for demons to hide in.

The main objective of the walk is the summit of Moel Famau, at 1817 feet (554m) the highest point of the Clwydian Hills. The Clwydian range is made up from shales and flagstones laid down in the Silurian period some 420 million years ago. Moel Famau means either 'the mother of mountains', because it is the highest hill in the range, or 'the mothers' mountain, perhaps because of some ancient connection with the worship of Celtic fertility goddesses. The hill looks most impressive when seen from the Vale of Clwyd to the west. The steep 1500 foot drop on this side is the result of a geological fault which was responsible for raising up the Clwydian Hills some 250 million years ago. In 1773 Moel Famau was reported to have erupted. The hill began to rumble and bellow at about eleven o' clock one night and an hour later a loud explosion was heard. The summit of the hill was split open and burning rocks were thrown out. As it is quite impossible that Moel Famau could erupt, the story is hard to account for – unless it was a hoax. The summit is adorned with the still substantial remains of an Egyptianate tower which was built between 1810 and 1812 to commemorate the 50th jubilee of George III's reign. About 5000 people attended the laying of the foundation stone on 25th October 1810. The crowd sang a version of 'God save the King' which had had an extra verse specially written for the occasion:

And as this joyous day
The joyous pile we lay
To Britain's King;
By love, by freedom led,
We'll rear its towering head,
Firm as its rocky bed,
To George our King.

When complete, the monument's head towered some 115 feet above the ground but its rocky bed was rather less than firm. To the delight of many locals, who regarded it as an eyesore, the tower collapsed after a storm in 1862. Even in its ruined state, however, the tower makes Moel Famau readily identifiable even in distant views.

One of the most striking features of the Clwydian range is its chain of six Iron Age hillforts, built between 400 and 200 BC. If they were all occupied at the same time, they must have given the hills the appearance of a prehistoric Maginot Line. Though none of these forts are visited on this walk, three of them, Moel Arthur, Moel y Gaer and Foel Fenlli, are prominent features of the views. A fourth, Penycloddiau, can also be seen to the north of Moel Arthur. When in use, the ramparts of these forts were surmounted by wooden palisades while the ditches and ramparts themselves would have been planted with brambles and blackthorn to make them almost impossible to cross. At Moel y Gaer, west of the summit of Moel Famau, the defences were further strengthened with stone spikes which projected out of the ramparts. Caches of stones for slings were kept on the ramparts in readiness for any attack. Excavations in some of the hillforts in the Clwyds have shown that there were dwelling huts, workshops and storehouses inside the ramparts but archaeologists are uncertain whether these fortified hilltop sites were permanently occupied or just used as refuges in times of trouble. One thing does seem certain; the Clwydian Hills in the Iron Age were a lot less peaceful than they are today. There are also many burial mounds on the slopes of Moel Famau, dating from the Neolithic and Bronze ages.

Moel Famau is a Site of Special Scientific Interest on account of its bird life. Kestrel, buzzard, raven and pied flycatchers are often seen. In the summer, look out for the rare ring ouzel. This is about the size of a blackbird and has a prominent white flash on its breast. It is most likely to be seen in gullies high on the flanks of the hills rather than on the open moorland and only in areas above 1000 feet above sea level. The birds like to fatten on rowan berries before migrating to north Africa in August.

The Walk

This is a straightforward hill walk with no route-finding problems and generally good conditions underfoot. There is about 1500 ft

(450m) of ascent in all, though only a few sections are really steep. This is one of the quieter routes up Moel Famau.

Start by walking past the church and turning left down a single track lane for 600 yards. Just after passing a small reedy pond, turn right off the lane and walk a few yards up the drive to Tyddyn-y-foel farm to a stone stile. Keep the hedge on your left through two fields to a junction between two bridleways. Take the branch which is more or less opposite. The bridleway goes uphill at an easy gradient and has a surface of stone chippings for the first 200 yards but this changes to grass after going through a gate below the earthen dam of a small reservoir. The bridleway was probably once hedged in but the hedges have long since gone to seed and it is now flanked by trees and hawthorn bushes. After ½ mile the track fords a small stream and the gradient gets noticeably steeper. The height above sea level is now about 1050 feet.

The bridleway ends about 200 yards further on at a stand of larches and a stony path continues steeply upwards through heather. However, the gradient eases after about 300 yards or so and the path crosses a bridleway and heads up alongside a Forestry Commission plantation. The summit monument soon comes into view and a short stiff climb brings you to the top. The view from the summit is excellent in clear weather, when the Snowdonian mountains can look surprisingly near. In exceptional conditions even the Isle of Man and the Lake District can be seen (not that I've ever been that lucky).

Leave the summit in a WNW direction along the Offa's Dyke path which is followed along the ridge of the Clwydian Hills for the next 2½ miles. There is a fence and wall on the right all of the way. The steep slopes down to the Vale of Clwyd and the Alyn valley make this an exhilarating walk at any time but it is especially good in late summer when the heather is in bloom, turning the hills purple. Though there are a few short uphill sections the trend of the ridge is generally downhill and steps have been built on the steeper parts to control erosion. After ½ mile the path turns north and a mile further on crosses a bridletrack at a high pass. A right turn here will take you back to Cilcain in about 2½ miles. However, the route

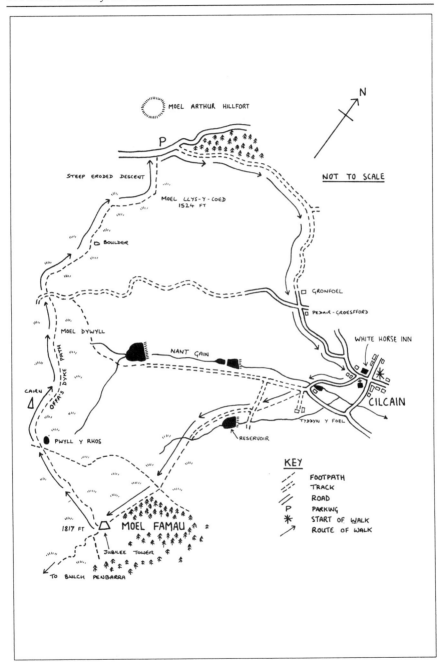

MOEL ARTHUR HILLFORT

STEEP ERODED DESCENT

MOEL LLYS-Y-COED
1524 FT

NOT TO SCALE

N

P

BOULDER

GRONFOEL

PEDAIR - GROESFFORD

WHITE HORSE INN

MOEL DYWYLL

NANT GAIN

OFFA'S DYKE PATH

CAIRN

CILCAIN

PWYLL Y RHOS

TYDDYN Y FOEL

RESERVOIR

KEY

FOOTPATH
TRACK
ROAD
P   PARKING
✳   START OF WALK
↗   ROUTE OF WALK

1817 FT   MOEL FAMAU

JUBILEE TOWER

TO BWLCH PENBARRA

continues gently uphill onto the summit of Moel Llys-y-coed. A large boulder passed on the ascent is a glacial erratic, carried here by an ice sheet and dumped when it melted at the end of the Ice Age. Beyond the summit, the path turns sharp left before plunging steeply down an eroded path to the road pass below the impressive hillfort on Moel Arthur.

At the road turn right for about 250 yards and turn right onto a gated track by a conifer plantation. At first the track runs alongside the plantation but after ½ mile it begins to run down into a dip, the views begin to open out and there is a great feeling of spaciousness about the scene. In May there is a profusion of bluebells on the banks of the track. At Gronfoel farm the track becomes a metalled lane. About 200 yards further on the lane comes to a crossroads: go straight ahead down the lane, which carries little traffic, and turn right at a T-junction about ½ mile further on to return to Cilcain after another 400 yards walking.

18. Around Neston and the Dee marshes

Distance: Allow 3½ hours for this 7 mile walk

Maps: Landranger 1:50,000 – 117; Pathfinder 1:25,000 – 756 (SJ 27/37)

Map reference of start/finish: SJ 289763

How to get there

From Chester: A540 for Hoylake, through the traffic lights at the junction with the A550, past the Puddington turn-off and then turn left at the next junction for Burton. At the T-junction turn left for Ness gardens, through the twee village of Burton, past Ness Gardens and a mile further on turn left at a modern brick church into Marshlands Road. Drive to the bottom of this road onto the edge of the marshes and park on the old spoil heaps to the right.

Public Transport: Walkers using public transport should start the walk from Neston town centre which can be reached on the frequent Crosville services 22 and 23 (Mon-Sat).

From Wrexham: A483 to Chester by-pass, east around Chester and out on the A41 Birkenhead road as far its junction with the A5117 at a roundabout (look out for the motel). Turn left for Queensferry, past the junction with the M56 and at the next roundabout turn right onto the A540 for Hoylake, through the traffic lights at the junction with the A550, past the Puddington turn-off and then turn left at the next junction for Burton. At the T-junction turn left for Ness gardens, through the twee village of Burton, past Ness gardens, and a mile further on turn left at a modern brick church into Marshlands Road. Drive to bottom of this road onto the edge of the marshes and park on the old spoil heaps to the right.

The Harp, Little Neston

An excellent, basic real-ale orientated small pub on the very edge of the Dee marshes. Opening hours are 11.00-23.00 Monday-Saturday and 12.00-15.00 and 19.00-22.30 on Sundays. Beers include cask conditioned Whitbread Trophy, Timothy Taylor's Landlord and

Weetwood Bitter. The pub serves a range of bar snacks at economical prices: available 11.00-21.00 Monday-Saturday, 12.00-15.00 and 19.00-21.00 on Sundays. There is a beer garden and children are allowed in the pub's back room but not in the bar. Walkers using the pub may leave their cars in the pub car park but must ask the landlord first. The pub was built c. 1711 as three dwelling houses. The building was turned into a pub between 1839 and 1852 to cater for coal miners at the nearby pit.

The Harp Inn, Little Neston

The Coach and Horses, Neston

A small town pub with a large beer garden about 100 yards off the Wirral Way. Families are welcome. Opening times are 11.00-23.00 Monday-Saturday and 12.00-15.00 and 19.00-22.30 on Sundays. Beers include cask conditioned Morlands Speckled Hen Bitter and regular guest beers. The pub serves a limited range of bar snacks and simple meals at economical prices through most of the day. The pub does not have a car park.

Background

Looking out from Neston or Parkgate over the vast flat expanses of waterlogged salt-marsh to the distant waters of the Dee, it is hard to imagine that these towns were once important ports. Neston was developed as a port in the mid 16th century by the City of Chester. Throughout the Middle Ages Chester had been the main port for Ireland but a combination of silting of the Dee and the introduction of bigger ships forced shipping to move downstream. By around 1700 Neston too had become silted up and traffic moved further downstream to Parkgate and until the 1820s the village was the terminus for the Dublin packet-boat service. William of Orange left from Parkgate on his way to win the Battle of the Boyne in 1690 and Handel stayed there in 1741 on his way to give the first performance of the Messiah in Dublin. Wirral folk were keen to take advantage of all this commercial traffic and earned themselves an unenviable reputation as wreckers, lighting misleading beacons at night to lure unsuspecting captains to sail their ships aground so that they could be robbed. Parkgate also became a fashionable seaside resort: one visitor was a local girl, Emma Lyon – better known as Lady Hamilton, Lord Nelson's mistress – who bathed here to cure a skin complaint in 1784. In the 1820s the Dublin packet moved to Holyhead after the completion of Telford's new London-Holyhead road (now the A5) and Parkgate went out of business as a port. Many of the old quays survive, though they are now high and dry, and are visited on this walk. Relics of an even older seafaring connection can be seen in Neston Church (easily visited by a short detour off-route) which has a collection of stone carvings with scenes of battle and the hunt produced by Viking settlers in the 10th century. Most of the settlers came from Norway and they quietly settled the Lake District and the Lancashire and Wirral coasts while Alfred the Great's successors had their hands full fighting the Danes of the Danelaw. Many Wirral place-names, for example those ending in 'by', show a Norse influence. Neston church itself is a handsome building. The walls of its medieval tower are immensely thick so, it is thought, that it could act as a refuge from pirates.

Though the salt-marshes look as if they have been there from time immemorial they are actually of very recent origin; most of those off Neston and Parkgate have appeared only since the 1930s and they are still spreading over the sands. In summer, the marshes are quiet apart from the larks but in winter huge flocks of wildfowl and waders frequent the Dee. Teal, mallard, widgeon, pintail and shelduck, oystercatcher, plover, knot, dunlin, redshank and curlew are all present but, as the birds spend most of their time feeding on the tidal mudflats, there are few places where they can easily be seen. High tide is the best time to look as then the birds are forced off the flats onto the shoreline. All the marshes north of Marshlands Road are owned and managed as a nature reserve by the RSPB.

This walk can, if desired, easily be combined with a visit to Ness Gardens. Construction of the gardens was started in 1898 by A. K. Bulley, a Liverpool cotton merchant and they are famous for their collections of rhododendrons, azaleas, cherries and heathers: they were donated to Liverpool University in 1948.

The Walk

This is an easy walk along mostly level well-maintained paths, bridleways and lanes. The marshland paths are wet in places, however. A long stretch of this walk is on the Wirral Way through the middle of Neston but apart from a short stretch through a housing estate you will hardly notice.

The walk starts from the weathered shale spoil heaps which are all that remains of Denhall colliery which operated from c. 1850 to 1928. Start by heading north on the clear path alongside the fence at the edge of the marshes. This is not actually a right of way but there are no access problems. After ¼ mile you come to a metal stile: once over it you are back on a public footpath. The ruined walls at the edge of the marsh around here are the remains of Neston Quay: when built in the 16th century they were busy with shipping but are now high and dry except for a little brook trickling through them. Cross this brook by stepping stones and continue on the path along the edge of the marsh. There are huge reed beds here and herons are common. About ½ mile from the old quay the path comes to an end at the edge of a housing estate – dense reed beds and waterlogged

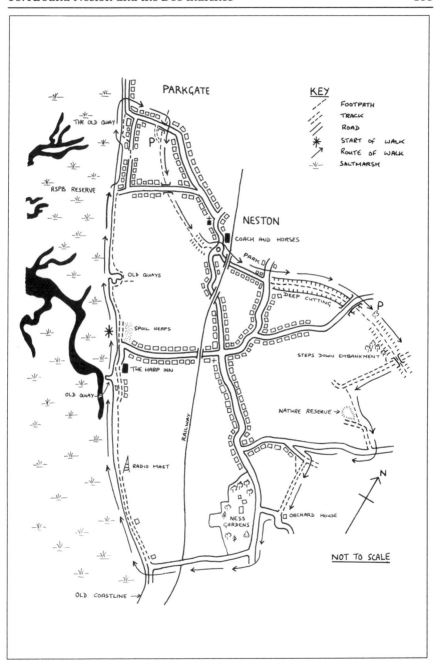

PARKGATE

KEY

Footpath
Track
Road
Start of walk
Route of walk
Saltmarsh

THE OLD QUAY

RSPB RESERVE

NESTON

COACH AND HORSES

OLD QUAYS

PARK

DEEP CUTTING

SPOIL HEAPS

STEPS DOWN EMBANKMENT

THE HARP INN

OLD QUAY

NATURE RESERVE →

RADIO MAST

N

ORCHARD HOUSE

NESS GARDENS

NOT TO SCALE

OLD COASTLINE →

RAILWAY

ground make further progress along the edge of the marshes impossible.

The path leads out onto Manorial Road, a residential street which you follow right to the end where a snicket (signpost 'The Parade') leads through into a roughly surfaced road lined by big houses. Where this road turns right, take another snicket between 'Riverside' and 'The Slipway' to bring you out on The Parade – Parkgate's promenade – at The New Quay, a gruesome modern pub in which most walkers would not feel at home. The Dublin packet boats used to leave from a quay opposite Mostyn Hall School (once a fashionable hotel) just 50 yards further up The Parade. Notice the two old pebble-dashed houses on the corner of Station Road: the one nearest the marsh (no. 16) is reputed to be where Lady Hamilton stayed during her visit in 1784. The house next door (no. 15) has the name Nelson set in black pebbles in front of it. This is a memorial not to Lady H's lover but to Nelson Burt, a boy who lived there and was drowned in the Mersey in 1822.

Turn right up Station Road and just past the cricket club walk up the entrance road on the right into the Wirral Country Park which has been created out of an old railway line closed in 1962. The route now follows the Wirral Way for the next two miles. At first the way goes along the old railway line, with occasional views opening up over the Dee estuary but after ¾ mile the way goes down the embankment to the right and onto a main road (Bridge St). Turn left and walk up to the mini-roundabout. Go straight on here if you want to visit the Coach and Horses (or Neston church), otherwise turn right into Station Road ('Wirral Way' signpost), under a railway bridge and straight on along the edge of a housing estate to reach a main road at a T-junction. Cross the road (Mellock Lane) and follow the path downhill into a deep gorge-like railway cutting. This is quite an atmospheric place, deeply shaded by trees overhead and hemmed in by mossy rock walls, though it can be wet underfoot. After about ½ mile you emerge from the cutting at a picnic area, blinking, probably, in the unaccustomed daylight.

The way continues along the old railway but now on an embankment lined with tangles of hawthorn, brambles and wild roses, through pasture land. After about 500 yards, at a wooden footbridge, go right down the embankment (sign 'Cuckoo Lane to Little Neston') to a muddy track and turn right. The track narrows after about 200 yards between bracken covered banks, becomes sandy and starts to climb uphill. At the top of the hill, where the track turns sharp right, cross a stile on the left. Good views now open out across to the Welsh hills. Follow the edge of the field to another stile and then along the edge of the Windle Hill nature reserve (an old tip with a large butterfly population in the summer) to come out on a rutted track. Turn left along the track to a gate onto a metalled lane and turn right. The lane sees a fair amount of traffic and is narrow in places to look out for cars. Six hundred yards down the lane turn left into Flashes Lane. This is metalled at first but just past the last house it turns into a grassy track. Turn right here onto a clear path across a patch of waste ground for about 100 yards to reach a sunken footpath. This footpath, which is quite badly overgrown in places and quite muddy after rain, brings you out at 'Orchard House' on a metalled lane.

Turn right here and follow the lane down to the main road almost opposite the entrance to Ness Gardens (opening hours 09.30-dusk March-October and 09.30-16.00 November-February (admission charge)). Follow the main road past the gardens – there is a footpath all the way – and turn right down Denhall Lane and follow it right down to the edge of the marshes. There are excellent views across the Dee estuary to Moel Famau from the lane. At the bottom of the lane, turn right and follow the lane along the marsh edge. The lane deteriorates into a rutted track after passing a radio station and then, a few hundred yards further on, through a gate, the track becomes a muddy path. Another 400 yards on, the path climbs up a bank, off the marshes and onto a roughly surfaced residential road, past an old quay, now high and dry, and the Harp Inn and so, another 200 yards further on, back to the old colliery.

19. Riverbanks and green lanes around Aldford

Distance: Allow 3½ hours for this 7 mile walk

Maps: Landranger 1:50,000 – 117; Pathfinder 1:26,000 – 790 (SJ 45/55), 774 (SJ 46/56)

Map reference of start/finish: SJ 418595

How to get there

From Chester: Aldford is about 5 miles south of Chester on the B5130. Turn right immediately after the road zigzags across the bridge over Aldford Brook into Church Lane. Park about ¼ mile down this lane by the church.

Public transport: Services C56, Chester to Wrexham, and C57, Chester to Whitchurch, both pass through Aldford at about three-hourly intervals (Mon-Sat).

From Wrexham: Leave Wrexham on the A534 and about ¾ mile after crossing the Dee at Holt, turn left onto the B5130 for about 3 miles to Aldford. Turn left just after passing the Grosvenor Arms into Church Lane and park near the church.

Public Transport: Service C56, Wrexham to Chester, passes through Churton and Aldford at about three-hourly intervals (Mon-Sat).

The Grosvenor Arms, Aldford

A large, late 19th century inn built by the Grosvenor estate to serve the village of Aldford and still owned by the estate. It has been attractively renovated. Opening hours are 11.30-14.30 and 17.00-23.00 Monday-Saturday, 12.00-15.00 and 19.00-22.30 on Sunday. Cask conditioned beers include Boddingtons and Buckley's Best and there are three guest beers, changed weekly. There is also an interesting range of imported bottled beers and an extensive wine list. Food is served 12.00-14.00 and 19.00-22.00 seven days. Menus are changed daily and there are different lunch-time and evening menus. A typical lunch-time menu includes filled baked potatoes, open sandwiches, smoked salmon, lobster thermidor, grills and steaks, cold chicken and ham pie and lamb curry. Evening menus tend to offer more substantial meals. The price range is a bit above average. The pub has a large beer garden and terrace where children are welcome at all times and at lunch-times children are also allowed in the conservatory and 'library'.

The Grosvenor Arms, Aldford

The White Horse, Churton

See walk 20 for details.

Background

Aldford is an attractive estate village, still largely owned by the Grosvenor estate – the seat of the dukes of Westminster – and tenanted by their employees. The village was largely rebuilt in the late Victorian era by the second marquess of Westminster in the distinctive style of Chester architect John Douglas. Most of the houses have large gardens where estate workers could grow their own vegetables and outbuildings to accommodate a cow, pigs and hens. The estate made grazing land and hay fields available for the cottagers. Though it must have cost them most of their leisure time, the cottagers were effectively self-sufficient in foodstuffs. One notable building, passed on this walk, is 'Stocks View' (opposite the village stocks). This house was originally built by the first duke in 1893, in a very progressive gesture for the time, as a home and dispensary for a district nurse. Sadly, the present duke is best known for his very unprogressive views on the public's rights of access to the countryside. The home of the dukes, Eaton Hall is just across the river from Aldford but all that can be seen of it from this walk is the Gothic clocktower (a mini Big Ben) of the family chapel, built in the 1880s. The hall itself, built in 1972, is a squat marble shoebox that wouldn't look out of place on an industrial estate. This is the third hall to stand on the site: it replaces a Victorian neo-Gothic extravaganza which was demolished after it became structurally unsound. Linking the hall to the village is a rather splendid iron bridge, which is, happily, a public right of way. The bridge, a graceful single arch, was built in 1824 for Robert Grosvenor, the first marquess of Westminster, by the engineer William Hazledine to a design of Thomas Telford. The bridge is built at the site of a ford, once crossed by the Roman road which linked Shrewsbury with the legionary fortress at Chester, from which the village gets its name, 'Old Ford'. The ford became unusable after the building of a weir in Chester raised the river level at Aldford. However, the outline of the ford is still said to be visible from the iron bridge when river levels are very low.

The ford was still important enough in Norman times to warrant the building of a large motte and bailey castle to defend it. The 'motte' of a motte and bailey castle is a large mound surrounded by a deep ditch which was topped with a wooden stockade and a watch-tower. In wartime this served the same function as the keep in a stone castle. The 'bailey' was a moated and stockaded enclosure adjoining the motte which held stables, workshops and living accommodation. Here at Aldford the motte is well-preserved and impressive but the bailey is less well-defined: it lay between the shallow ditches running between the motte and the church. Motte and bailey castles are commonly thought of as being temporary fortifications which were thrown up quickly when trouble threatened and soon abandoned when things calmed down. However, recent excavations have shown that many of them continued in use for well over a century after they were built and that they were constantly maintained and modified.

Parts of this walk follow the route of the Marches Way, an unofficial long-distance footpath running 204 miles from Chester to Cardiff.

Iron bridge over the Dee at Aldford

The Walk

If desired, this walk can be combined with Walk 20 to make a round walk of about 11 miles.

This is an easy walk on riverside paths and green lanes with no route-finding problems. However, by late summer parts of the riverside path become badly overgrown with nettles.

Start the walk at the wooden gate by the church tower (Marches Way route marker). Cross the field, past the remains of the motte and bailey castle, to a kissing gate, then through a small metal gate and across to a wooden gate in the field corner. This brings you onto a metalled drive leading to Eaton Hall. Turn left and follow the drive for a few yards down an avenue of drab rhododendrons to the blue and white painted iron bridge over the Dee. The path goes left from the bridge along the river bank, at first through yew trees and then a long open field. After a long ½ mile you will come to an overgrown gate which brings you onto a rutted track. Turn right and follow the track along the edge of a wood back to the riverbank.

Follow the river round a wide loop and after about a mile you will come to a swampy marl pit. The right of way here sticks to the riverbank, passing between the pit and the river, but it is so over-grown with nettles in late summer that it is not easy to see the path (the nettles are easily avoided by going left and skirting around the edge of the pit, through a gap in the hedge, and back to the riverbank). About 300 yards further on the path enters a very long thin field which is part of a circuit used for training racehorses. At the far end this field widens out as the training circuit swings away to the left. Go through the gate in the right-hand corner of the field and turn left, away from the river bank, on a rutted track along the edge of a wood. At the end of the wood, continue straight on with a hedge to the left and an area of marshland to the right. About ½ mile after leaving the riverbank the track brings you back to it again, at a pale green painted chalet. Cross the stile by the chalet (public footpath sign), through a field, across another stile, past a white painted chalet ('Noonday') and into a young plantation of ash and alder. Continue for a little over a hundred yards and turn sharp left off the riverbank just past a large old oak tree onto a grassy track. The track runs through the plantation at first, then at a metal gate it becomes an attractive hedged-in green lane. The lane climbs very gently uphill for about ¾ mile to come out onto a metalled road.

Carry on straight ahead down the road (Hob Lane) to come out onto the B5130 at the White Horse Inn. Cross the road, go down Pump Lane (signposted to Coddington) and after about 200 yards turn left into a one-way street just opposite an attractive half tim-

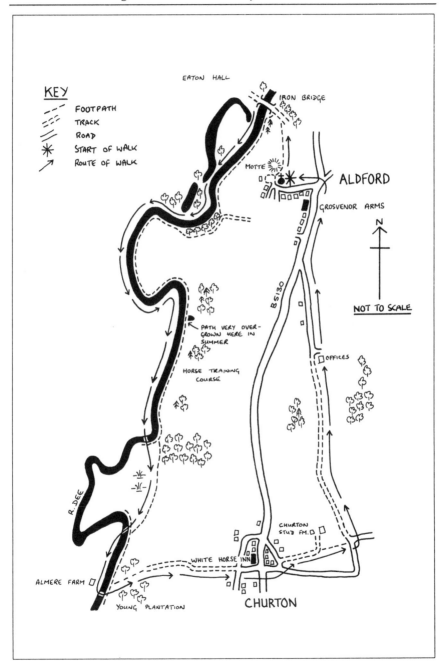

bered house. A few yards up this road turn right into the drive to Churton Stud Farmhouse (public footpath and Marches Way signs). Where the drive turns sharp left up towards the farm, go straight on and cross the stile marked with the Marches Way sign onto a path fenced in along the side of a hedge. Follow this to a footbridge over a shallow brook, then across a narrow field to a metal gate and onto a metalled lane.

Turn sharp left here onto a green lane. This is muddy in places but is mostly easy going and the next mile is straightforward pleasant walking through pastures and crop land with good views of the Peckforton Hills to the east. At a farm which has been converted into offices, the green lane becomes a quiet metalled lane which you follow for about 700 yards to its junction with the B5130 just outside Aldford. Turn right and walk down the B5130 (footpaths on both sides of the road), past the junction with Rushmere Lane, to the Grosvenor Arms. Just past the Grosvenor Arms, the village stocks can be seen on the right-hand side of the road. Just opposite them is Stocks View, the old district nurse's house and surgery. Turn left here into Church Lane and so, shortly, back to the church.

---

20. Churton, the river Dee and Farndon bridge

Distance: Allow 2½ hours for this 4¾ mile walk

Maps: Landranger 1:50,000 – 117; Pathfinder 1:25,000 – 789 (SJ 25/35), 790 (SJ 45/55)

Map reference of start/finish: SJ 417565

How to get there

From Chester: Churton is 7 miles south of Chester on the B5130. The White Horse Inn is prominently sited on the left-hand side of the main road at the crossroads in the centre of Churton. Walkers not intending to visit the pub can find limited parking at the bottom of Hob Lane: to reach it turn right at the White Horse Inn.

Public transport: Services C56, Chester to Wrexham, and C57, Chester to Whitchurch, both pass through Churton at about three-hourly intervals (Mon-Sat).

From Wrexham: Take the A534 Nantwich road and, unless you want to start the walk from Farndon, by-pass Holt and turn left onto the B5130 after crossing the Dee. Churton is 1½ miles north of the junction and the White Horse Inn is situated on the left at the crossroads in the centre of the village. Walkers not intending to use the pub will find limited room for parking at the bottom of Hob Lane: to reach it turn left at the White Horse Inn.

Public transport: Service C56, Wrexham to Chester, passes through Farndon and Churton at about three-hourly intervals (Mon-Sat).

The White Horse Inn, Churton

A large, comfortable pub which welcomes walkers. Opening hours are 11.30-15.00 and 18.00-23.00 Monday-Friday, 11.00-23.00 Saturday and 12.00-15.00 and 19.00-22.30 Sunday. Beers include cask conditioned Bass, Worthington's bitter, Forshaw's bitter and Stone's bitter. There is an extensive and very varied menu of snacks and main meals. Roast lunches are served on Sundays. Food is available 12.00-14.30 and 18.30-21.00 Monday-Sunday. Morning coffee can be booked for parties (01829-270208). There is a beer garden but children are welcome in the pub. Walkers using the pub may leave their cars in the car park. Dogs are allowed in the public bar. The present building was built in 1908 to replace a small thatched cottage village inn on the same site.

The Nags Head, Farndon

A friendly ex-coaching inn. Opening hours are 11.30-15.00 and 17.30-23.00 Monday-Saturday, 12.00-15.00 and 19.00-22.30 Sunday. Beers include cask conditioned Marston's Pedigree and bitter, Banks' mild and regular guest beers. The pub serves a range of snacks and main meals from 12.00-14.00 and 19.00-21.30 Monday-Sunday. Children are welcome in the lounge. Walkers using the pub are welcome to leave their cars in the car park; please ask first.

The Nags Head, Farndon

Background

The highlight of this walk is the sturdy nine arched sandstone bridge over the Dee, linking the villages of Farndon and Holt. The bridge, built sometime between 1315 and 1397, is the object of a certain amount of (understandable) local possessiveness and is known as Holt bridge or Farndon bridge, depending upon which side of the river one lives. During the Civil War, the bridge was the object of the much more bitter rivalry of king and Parliament. Holt castle was a royalist stronghold and the bridge was fortified with a gatehouse and garrisoned by Royalist troops. Late in 1643 a force of 2000 Lancashire and Cheshire Roundheads under Sir William Brereton occupied Farndon and prepared to assault the bridge. On the 9th November Brereton launched a diversionary attack downstream drawing off many of the Royalists while the main force stormed the bridge, bombarding the defenders with hand grenades until they fled. However, Holt castle held out against the Roundheads until the bridge was recaptured for the king by Prince Rupert in 1645.

Bridge over the River Dee at Farndon

The bridge is reputed to be haunted by the ghosts of two children, the heirs of the Welsh prince Gruffyth ap Madog, who were supposedly thrown from the bridge to their deaths by their guardian, earl John de Warrenne, so that he could claim their inheritance. The story is certainly untrue and was probably invented to explain the transfer of the lordship of Holt from Madog's heirs to the English earl following Edward I's conquest of the Principality in 1282.

Farndon's 14th century parish church suffered serious fire damage in the Civil War battles and had to be almost completely rebuilt in 1658. In 1662 William Barnston, a local Royalist landowner, commissioned a stained glass window for the family's side chapel to commemorate the Royalist defenders of Chester. It shows Royalist officers and soldiers in the dress and equipment of the day and is thought to be the only stained glass window in the country which has the Civil War as a theme.

A quite different point of interest on this walk is the Aquafarm ecological fish farm on the riverside between Farndon and Churton. The farm produces carp, geese, watercress, herbs and reeds for thatching in an ingenious system which uses the waste products from one lifeform as nourishment for another lifeform so that no waste or pollution is produced. The water system is self-contained and the circulation is maintained only by gravity and a wind pump: the only external input into the system is manure. The manure is fed into a small pond where it forms a nutrient-rich (and no doubt highly flavoured) broth for microscopic animals called zooplankton and midge larvae which are used to feed the carp. The water in this pond would be lethal to fish life so it has to be cleaned. To do this, it is first filtered through reed beds which absorb all of the 'nasties' except ammonia. Then the water is trickled through beds of watercress. Bacterial nodes on the roots of watercress convert the ammonia into nitrates which the plant uses for growth. The water is now safe to drink and is run into the fish ponds. Geese are bred on the fish ponds where they keep grass and weeds under control and their droppings provide extra nutrients for zooplankton. Pest control on the farm is also completely ecological. To combat the problem of greenfly infestation of the reeds, fennel (itself saleable) and marigolds are grown to attract hoverfly: they lay eggs on the reeds and their larvae eat the greenfly. The farm is not normally open to the public but there is a public viewing area and tours can be arranged for organised parties – contact the owner Roy Watkins, 01829-270713.

The Walk

If desired this walk can be combined with walk 19 to make a round walk of about 11 miles.

The walk starts in the small village of Churton. In the course of this century it has changed, like so many Cheshire villages, from being an agricultural community to a dormitory for commuters. Set off by walking down Hob Lane at the side of the pub. Where the lane turns left, carry straight on down a rutted cart track for about ½ mile and through a gate into a young plantation of alder. There are good views across to the Clwydian Hills but the river itself is invisible behind trees. Carry on to the river bank, where there was once a ferry, and turn left, leaving the plantation behind after passing the first of the many weekenders' chalets which lie on both sides of the river. Keep to the river bank for another half mile to where the course of the river turns sharply to the right. The path leaves the field and goes through a rather overgrown patch of riverbank to emerge onto an unsurfaced road. Immediately opposite is a gate with a 'Private, no parking' notice on it. Go through this gate, it is a right of way, and walk along the field edge to come back onto the river bank again – you have cut across the neck of a half-mile meander.

Cross the stile here into the grounds of the fish farm and follow the way markers round to the right, past the wildlife viewing area (open to the public to use) and at the green hatching shed turn right, up a few steps, through a gate and onto the river bank again. The route to Farndon is now simple: except where riverside chalets get in the way, just keep to the river bank which, in summer, has a large population of iridescent blue damselflies. Horse races were held in these flat riverside fields until the 19th century. About a mile from the fish farm the first of the red sandstone cliffs which line the Dee at Farndon comes into sight. These cliffs have been designated a site of special geological interest on account of the striking examples of current bedding which they show (on this, see the background notes to walk 1). These geological formations are best seen on the cliffs above the car park by Farndon's impressive nine-arched medieval bridge, where there is an interpretational notice board. From the bridge take the path which starts behind the interpretational notice board, up a flight of stone steps to the top of the cliffs. Though the clifftop vegetation is quite dense it is possible to get a good aerial view of the bridge from here. After about 100 yards, turn left onto a path which runs at first along a wooden fence and then along the side of a graveyard to an iron gate by the church tower. Bear right around the church and leave the church yard by the east gate. Keep straight ahead down the road, past a health centre, to its junction with a main road.

Opposite is Walkers Lane to the right of a black and white house. Go down the lane and out into fields with good views of the Peckforton Hills and Beeston Castle to the east. At first the path keeps close to the field edges but soon the fields become bigger and more open while the path is often obscured by ploughing. However, the route always keeps to the same northerly line to come out on the Farndon-Churton road after about ¾ mile. On the way there is a good view of the Barnston memorial, an obelisk commemorating Major Roger Barnston, from the local landowning family, who was fatally wounded at the siege of Lucknow in 1857 during the Indian Mutiny. On reaching the road turn left and about 200 yards further on turn right into the quiet lane which leads back to Churton and the start of the walk.

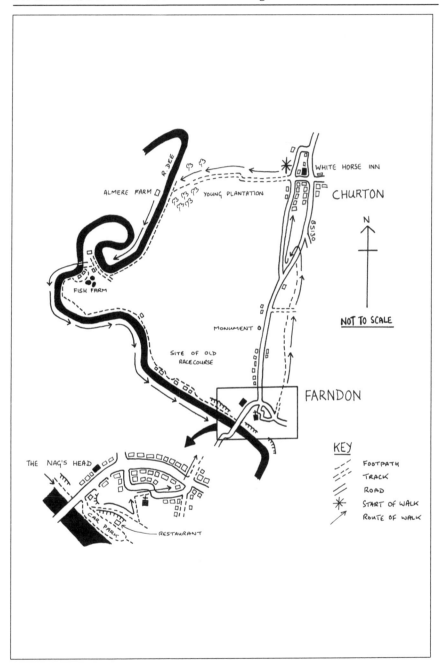

We publish guides to individual towns, plus books on walking and cycling in the great outdoors throughout England and Wales. This is a recent selection:

Country Walking

EAST CHESHIRE WALKS – Graham Beech *(£5.95)*

WEST CHESHIRE WALKS – Jen Darling *(£5.95)*

TEA SHOP WALKS IN CHESHIRE – Clive Price *(£6.95)*

TEA SHOP WALKS IN THE LAKE DISTRICT – Jean Patefield *(£6.95)*

TEA SHOP WALKS IN THE CHILTERNS – Jean Patefield *(£6.95)*

MOSTLY DOWNHILL IN THE PEAK DISTRICT – Clive Price *(£6.95)*
(two volumes, White Peak & Dark Peak)

HILL WALKS IN MID WALES – Dave Ing *(£8.95)*

WELSH WALKS: Dolgellau /Cambrian Coast – L. Main & M. Perrott *(£5.95)*

WELSH WALKS: Aberystwyth & District – L. Main & M. Perrott *(£5.95)*

WALKS IN MYSTERIOUS WALES – Laurence Main *(£7.95)*

RAMBLES IN NORTH WALES – Roger Redfern *(£6.95)*

PUB WALKS IN SNOWDONIA – Laurence Main *(£6.95)*

BEST PUB WALKS IN GWENT – Les Lumsdon *(£6.95)*

PUB WALKS IN POWYS – Les Lumsdon & Chris Rushton *(£6.95)*

BEST PUB WALKS IN PEMBROKESHIRE – Laurence Main *(£6.95)*

RAMBLES AROUND MANCHESTER – Mike Cresswell *(£5.95)*

LAKELAND WALKING: On The Level – Norman Buckley *(£6.95)*

FIFTY CLASSIC WALKS IN THE PENNINES – Terry Marsh *(£8.95)*

WEST PENNINE WALKS – Mike Cresswell *(£5.95)*

BEST PUB WALKS AROUND CENTRAL LONDON – Ruth Herman *(£6.95)*

BEST PUB WALKS IN ESSEX – Derek Keeble *(£6.95)*

More Pub Walks . . .

There are many more titles in our fabulous series of 'Pub Walks' books for just about every popular walking area in the UK, all featuring access by public transport. We label our more recent ones as 'best' to differentiate them from inferior competitors!